GROW YOUR OWN FAMILY TREE

A Comprehensive Guide to Tracing Your Ancestry

REVISED EDITION

Pauline Golds

Emerald Guides
www.straightforwardbooks.co.uk

Emerald Guides

© Pauline Golds 2023 – Revised Edition

Pauline Golds has asserted the moral right to be identified as the author of this work.

All rights reserved. No part of this publication may be reproduced in a retrieval system or transmitted by any means, electronic or mechanical, photocopying or otherwise, without the prior permission of the copyright holders.

ISBN 978-1-80236-172-8

Printed by 4edge www.4edge.co.uk

Cover design by Pauline Golds/BW Studio Derby

Original images by Mikey Jackson www.mikeyjackson.com

Whilst every effort has been made to ensure that the information contained within this book is correct at the time of going to press, the author and publisher can take no responsibility for the errors or omissions contained within.

This Book is Dedicated to my Family

Those who have long since passed into the Silent Land, those who have travelled beside me along the way and those who are yet to begin the journey.

CONTENTS

Preface	ix

Chapter 1. What Resources Are Available? — 1
Begin at the beginning — 1
The Internet — 2
Family history societies — 5
Archives and libraries — 6

Chapter 2. Birth, Marriage and Death – Part 1 — 8
Getting started — 8
Birth, marriage and death certificates — 10
Recording your research — 13

Chapter 3. Censuses — 17
About the censuses — 17
Obtaining the censuses — 21
Adding to your research — 26

Chapter 4. Birth, Marriage and Death – Part 2 — 28
How were these events recorded before 1837? — 28
Obtaining parish records — 33
What do parish records look like? — 38
Adding to your research — 38

Chapter 5. The Class System and Occupations — 44

Early forms of society in England — 44
Victorian society — 50
Obtaining records that give clues to your ancestor's occupation and social class — 54
How did your ancestor's occupation fit into the social hierarchy? — 57

Chapter 6. The Military — 58

The Royal Navy — 58
The British Army — 59
The Royal Air Force — 60
Obtaining military records — 63

Chapter 7. Crime in the 18th and 19th Centuries — 66

A brief history of crime in Victorian England — 66
Obtaining criminal records — 70

Chapter 8. The Poor Laws and the Workhouse — 73

Early Poor Laws — 74
The new Poor Laws and the Workhouse — 78
Obtaining Poor Law and Workhouse records — 82

Chapter 9. Death and Disease — 83

The Middle Ages — 83
The 16th to 18th Centuries — 88
The Industrial Revolution — 90
The 20th Century — 93
Obtaining information about the diseases and deaths of your ancestors — 96

CONTENTS

Chapter 10. Education and Apprenticeships   100

The history of education in Britain   101
Education for the disabled   104
Apprenticeships   106
Obtaining information about education and apprenticeships   110

Chapter 11. Geographical Mobility and Population Growth   114

General overview   114

Chapter 12. Scotland and Ireland   120

Scotland   120
Ireland   126

Chapter 13. American Research   129

General overview   129
Convicts sent to America   131
Religious 'Freedom' in America – Quakers, Pilgrims and Puritans   133
Economic Migrants   137
Slavery   138
Finding Birth, Marriage and Death Records   139
US Censuses   140
Other Useful Resources   140

Chapter 14. Canadian Research   142

General overview   142
Convicts Transported to Canada   145
Home Children   145

Slavery 147
Where to Find Canadian Records 149

Chapter 15. Caribbean Research — 151

General overview 151
The 'first' Caribbeans 151
European Dominance 152
Servants and White Slaves 153
Transportation 153
Pirates 154
The African Slave Trade 155
Asian immigrants 156
Researching your Caribbean Roots 157

Chapter 16. Europe — 160

General overview 160

In Conclusion — 162

Index 163

PREFACE

Some time ago, when I found myself hurtling toward the grand old age of fifty, I began, for the first time, to feel mortal. It was about this time that the BBC series "Who Do You Think You Are?" was first aired and one of the first celebrities to participate was the actress Amanda Redman, who had been in my class at school. This got me thinking about my own ancestors. I realised that I didn't even know the Christian names of my grandparents or my grandmothers' maiden names! Fortunately for me, the wonderful World Wide Web had now taken a firm foothold and it was possible to find these things out. Unfortunately for me, my parents had both passed away and I had lost all contact with elderly aunts and uncles, so I didn't have much of a starting point.

However, with patience and determination over the next couple of years I spent a lot of my spare time delving into that strange country they call the past, or at least the areas of it that were graced by my ancestors.

I discovered chimney sweeps and gamekeepers, blacksmiths and agricultural labourers, fishmongers and midwives to name but a few. I uncovered dark secrets of illegitimacy and crime and sad tales of poverty and the workhouse. I suppose when I began, I was hoping to find I was descended from an Earl or a famous scientist, perhaps even a renowned actress, but it wasn't to be. Like the majority of people from Britain's past, my ancestors were working class. They were poor, illiterate and they often met with disease and early death. I think by learning all of this, not only did it connect me to my ancestors, but it also made me thankful that I was born in the second half of the 20th century and did not have to endure the hardships of the past.

Since tracing my own family tree (and it is an ongoing project as more and more resources become available), I have had the pleasure of discovering the ancestors of friends and extended family, many of whom said to me "You should do this for a living!" So, I did, and the rest is history.

I now want to help others on their own voyage into the past. Hiring a professional is not always an option, but with time and patience and a few tips on the dos and don'ts, it *is* possible to Grow Your Own Family Tree.

In the first edition of this book, I focused solely on the British Isles. In the second edition I took a wider approach and included the U.S.A., Canada, the Caribbean and Europe. This revised edition brings the research bang up to date.

Good Luck and I hope your journey is as exciting and enlightening as mine.

Pauline Golds
2023

CHAPTER 1

What Resources are Available?

Begin at the Beginning

Many people think that the first place to start researching your family tree is by visiting some dusty old archive or by logging on to the internet. WRONG.

Your research should begin at home, firstly with yourself. You may think that the knowledge you already have is all there is, but might there be some old documents you have inherited lying in the back of a drawer somewhere? What about old photographs? Perhaps you have seen photographs in old albums and have not known who they are, but perhaps if you take them out of the album, some thoughtful ancestor might have written a name or even a date on the reverse.

Whilst we are on this subject, this is a must for all those who want to pass on information to future generations.

When you have a spare moment, go through all your photographs and write names and dates on the back in pencil. This could prove invaluable to those trying to trace *you* some day.

Anyway, I digress. After you have exhausted all possible avenues of research in your own home, then is the time to contact all the relatives. Older generations are particularly useful, but siblings, cousins and even nieces and nephews may hold some key information that they have, either as documents or as memories of tales long past told to them.

Once you have gathered everything you possibly can, then it's time to move on.

One more word of advice here, always work methodically. Start with one surname and if possible continue with that line until you have exhausted all your options. Then move on to the next surname, working chronologically back in time.

The Internet

Most people nowadays have a home computer, but if you don't have access to one, then it's not always a problem. Many libraries offer online access. Often this is free, and they usually give assistance to those who are novices in IT.

There is a huge amount of information online now, and that information is growing all the time. However, with so much around, it can be daunting knowing where to begin. Most websites charge a subscription or a 'pay as you go' method and the costs can mount up if you don't use them wisely.

WHAT RESOURCES ARE AVAILABLE

I have two personal favorites that I have ongoing subscriptions with: ancestry.com and findmypast.co.uk. (From hereon I shall refer to these sites as 'Ancestry' and 'Find my Past'). Since I wrote the original edition of this book in 2016, Ancestry and Find My Past have added millions of new records. Several more county Parish records are now available as well as military, criminal, medical – the list goes on.

These sites offer a range of payment options. Most websites, including these two, offer a free trial for a limited time, and this is the best way to start. If you like what you find, then it is probably best to begin with a monthly subscription (if this is an option), and once you are certain you intend to proceed in your quest, upgrade to an annual if funds allow. It always works out cheaper in the long run to purchase the longer alternative.

Also, it probably goes without saying that if you are not aware of any ancestors that hail from other countries, then just stick to the packages that offer UK records. You can always upgrade later if the need arises. Some websites such as thegenealogist.co.uk offer various levels of subscription within the UK records. This can sometimes be frustrating because just as you think you have found something of interest, it tells you that you can access it only if you upgrade. However, you may find that its tiered system gives more choice in your chosen search, so it may be the one for you.

If a website offers a subscription, then it is almost always preferable to the 'pay as you go' alternative. At first these may seem better value, but you often find yourself paying for false leads. Subscriptions allow you unlimited access to the records, so no matter how many times you reach a dead end, at least you have only wasted a little time, not money.

There are many very good websites that are free, and it is well worth making full use of these. I particularly recommend freereg.org.uk, freecen.org.uk, freebmd.org.uk and familysearch.org. Sites that you pay for usually have a mixture of original document images and transcripts. The downside of free websites is that they are invariably only transcripts, not images of original documents. Most transcripts will be accurate copies of original documentation, but it must be remembered that they have been transcribed by human beings, often volunteers, and human beings are prone to occasional errors. Some documents are hundreds of years old, faded, chewed by church mice and written in a hand very unlike our own, so even the most experienced transcriber can sometimes get it wrong.

Therefore, as far as possible always source your information from original documentation. You will find that the more often you look at the old and barely legible images, the more accustomed you will become to deciphering them. I suppose what I am trying to say here is, by all means use what others have done for you, but always double check where possible and trust your own judgement.

One very important word of warning here that I cannot emphasise enough is do not treat other people's research as written in stone. Many websites allow you to build your family tree and put it online for others to see. When I first began, I often took names from these trees, and it led me on many a wild goose chase. Many people rush in headfirst, see a name that looks a bit like what they want it to look like and add it to their tree. Always check this information for yourself. If you can't find it, then ask yourself "How did they find it?" Often you can contact the person through a message and ask them their source. My advice would be, if they don't answer, then disregard the information.

If looking for particular records such as apprenticeship or bastardy documents, a very useful website is genguide.co.uk which gives useful guides as to which sources offer what information.

Finally, occasionally it can be worth just typing an ancestor's name and possibly a few details directly into a search engine. This can be especially useful if your ancestor had an unusual name. My great-great grandfather's name was Cephas Tree and just by typing his name into Google I discovered a lead to a newspaper article outlining the story of when he and his daughter were condemned to hang for burglary. I was then able to find the original story in local newspapers in the East Sussex Records Office. (More about him in Chapter 7).

Family History Societies

Most counties and/or areas have Family History Societies and Groups that can prove to be invaluable, but once again they vary greatly in their usefulness. Most charge a yearly subscription of between £10 and £15 and for that you usually get a quarterly magazine. What you get in addition is where they differ. Some, like my own county Sussex, give free access to all pre-1837 baptisms and burials and a wide choice of CDs to purchase with other useful information such as marriages and monumental inscriptions. Others will look up information in their local archives either for free or for a fee. The key here is to look carefully into what they can offer you. If it is not totally clear on their website, email them to find out exactly what you can expect for your money.

If the Society you are interested in is close enough to you, you may be interested in local meetings and events that they hold. Here you can often pick up tips from others, both amateur and professional. Also, they often arrange trips to local or National Archives and can help you with your research there. The Federation of Family History Societies may help you find the Society that could be most useful to you and provide you with other practical information. Their website is http://ffhs.org.uk. A final note, if the Society is not in your area and you are just interested in obtaining baptism, marriage and burial records, don't forget that in some cases the information is on their websites, so always check them out first before you join up to a Society.

Archives and Libraries

When I first began my quest to trace my family tree, I assumed, as many people do, that my first port of call to find original parish records would be in the parishes themselves. I had an idea that I would be trekking around towns and villages, talking to the local clergymen and looking through dusty old documents that had been held in the same location for hundreds of years – WRONG.

Very few churches still keep their original records. They are mostly deposited in local archives and records offices. Many have been scanned and uploaded onto computers or at the very least have been copied onto microfilm or microfiche which are available to view when you visit.

Archives and other repositories hold a wealth of information that is not yet available on websites. The National Archives holds millions of records many of which can now be searched and even downloaded online. A visit to the County Records Office is also often very fruitful. However, it is always best to register with them first and check exactly what documents they hold. As you delve deeper into your family history, you may be looking for more personal details than just names and dates. Local resources are often more likely to hold what you are looking for.

County Records Offices almost always offer a look-up service for you which could save you travel costs. However, many of them charge a very high hourly rate with no guarantee of success, so be careful when considering using their services.

As well as County Archives there are many other repositories that hold useful information. I have found that sometimes County Libraries give a much more personal and cheaper online service. The rule is to always email or ring first to find out exactly what they can offer you. Sometimes the websites are a little ambiguous so if you are not sure – ask.

CHAPTER 2

Birth, Marriage and Death – Part 1

Getting Started

The first thing to do once you have gathered together all the documentation and noted memories of family members is to get organised.

Write down everything as you go, either in a Word document on the computer or on paper. Working on the computer is almost always preferable because changes can be made, and information added without the need for crossings out or rewrites. Printers are really cheap these days and well worth investing in if you don't already have one. (Do be aware though that ink is not usually cheap. In the course of my work, I probably spend more on ink in a couple of months than I spent on my printer in the first place).

Most printers now come with a scanner which can also be very useful. I think it adds to the presentation of your research if photographs of your ancestors are included on the page that details their information. I also like to add old images of places where they lived to get a feel for their surroundings.

Once you are certain that you have all the information available, then print it out. Whichever way you decide to record your work, always keep it stored neatly in a folder, filed in order. Use subject dividers for each surname and place certificates and other documents in punched plastic wallets.

Always try to work on one ancestor at a time, working backwards through that line until you reach a dead end. (These dead ends are not always permanent. Periodically going back to previous research can sometimes offer new leads when fresh information becomes available).

It is important to always reference your sources. This is most easily done using footnotes. If doing this with Word, place your cursor next to the fact that you want referenced, then simply click on the 'References' tab on the tool bar at the top of the page, and then click on footnotes and add your reference.

It is common for people to start their research with either their mother or their father. You probably know their date of birth, so this is the starting point. If you have their birth certificate it can supply you with information you may not be aware of, such as their father's occupation or their mother's maiden name. Of course, you may already know these facts and some, such as the father's occupation, are interesting but not vital to further the research.

If you are lucky, you will have information about what occurred before 1921. This is when the last available census is viewable, and this will be covered in the next chapter.

Birth, Marriage and Death Certificates

In this section I am referring to British records.

The chances are though, that you will not have earlier information, so obtaining birth certificates may be vital. Since 1837 in England and Wales (1855 in Scotland and 1864 in Ireland) it has been a legal requirement for every birth, marriage and death to be officially registered and certificates of proof issued. For England and Wales, these certificates are now available to order from the Government Record Office. (For Scotland and Ireland see the relevant chapter). There are several ways to find the certificate you wish to order. If you have not yet subscribed to any of the general websites, you should be able to find details at freebmd.org.uk. Simply type in as many details as you can e.g., name, year of birth, district of birth, and hit the 'find' button. One thing to remember is that towns within the boundaries of registration districts vary over time and are sometimes quite surprising. If you are looking for a fairly common name, it may be worth checking that you have the right district. This information is available on genuki.org.uk.

If you have already subscribed to a general website such as Ancestry or Find my Past, then these indexes are also available there. They will give you the information you need to order the certificate. That is the District, the Quarter of the year, the Volume no. and the Page no. Since September 1911, the mother's maiden name has also appeared in the index and this may be all you need to further your research. If this is the case, then you may be able to avoid buying the certificate at least at this stage.

You may find that you have all the information you need from online parish records (see Chapter 4), but if you do need or want to purchase the certificate, do not fall into the trap of ordering it from one of the ancestry websites. It is much cheaper to order it directly from gro.gov.uk.

At the time of writing, these certificates cost £11.00 each. Some are also available as pdf downloads for £7. You will need to register with the site then simply fill in the information and pay by debit or with a credit card.

The certificates take about two weeks to arrive (slightly quicker for the downloads) and will give you the following information:

- The name, date and place of birth.
- The father's name (if a father is recorded) and occupation.
- The mother's name, maiden surname and, after 1984, occupation.
- After 1969 the parents' places of birth are also recorded.

Once you have the birth certificate, it will give you all the information you need to order their parents' marriage certificate. The references can be found, and the documents ordered in exactly the same way as before.

Marriage certificates give you:

- The date and place of marriage.
- The name, age and marital status of the parties.
- Their occupation and address.
- The name and occupation of each party's father.
- The names of the witnesses.
- The name of the person who solemnised the marriage.

Death certificates, although not always necessary, can prove interesting reading. I tend to have a rather morbid curiosity about causes of death, particularly if they died young.

Death certificates give you:

- The name, date and place of death.
- The date and place of birth (prior to 1969 a certificate only showed the age of deceased).
- The occupation and usual address.
- The cause of death.
- The person who gave the information for the death registration.

Sometimes certificates give you surprising clues. For example, you may not be entirely sure that you have the right person, but perhaps the names of the witnesses are members of the same family or even neighbours (something you can check on the censuses).

It can sometimes be frustrating when there are several possibilities in the indexes. On occasion you may need to buy more than one certificate before you get the right one. Therefore, it is important to gather as much information as you can from other sources. For example, censuses can give ages, middle names and places of birth, all of which can narrow down the search.

I always find it useful to scan my certificates, so that I have a copy in my online records as well as a hard copy.

Finally, if you are looking for information regarding someone who was adopted, then check out www.adoptionsearchreunion.org.uk. It wasn't until 1927 that the official registration of adoptions was introduced in England (1930 in Scotland and 1931 in Northern Ireland). Prior to this, children were privately adopted, and they may have never known. Some were adopted out by charities like Dr. Barnardos and if you have an idea that this is the case, then it may be worth contacting the relevant organisation.

Recording Your Research

After you have made that initial search over the last hundred or so years, your work may look something like this:

Mother – <u>Jane Smith</u>

Jane was born on the 14th of July 1942 at 3 New Street, Brighton, Sussex.

She married William Thomas Jones on 4th May 1968 at Brighton Register Office.

At the time of her marriage she was living at 40 Shakespeare Road, Brighton.

Jane and William had two children; Geoffrey Stephen born on 22nd July 1970 and Jason John born on 17th July 1973. Both were born in Shoreham-by Sea, East Sussex.

Jane died of cancer on the 30th of December 2004 in Brighton General Hospital.

Grandfather – <u>John Smith</u>

John was born on the 5th of January 1904 at 15 Oakham Street, Brighton.

He married Anne Thomas on the 12th of July 1928 in St Peter's Church, Brighton

According to his marriage certificate John was a General Labourer.

On his daughter Jane's marriage certificate in 1968 it states he was a Factory Worker.

John died of chronic bronchitis on the 15th December 1978 at 17 Factory Road, Brighton.

BIRTH, MARRIAGE AND DEATH – PART 1

Don't forget to reference all your sources.

One last thing I would like to mention here is the option to create a chart for your family tree, which is something that you may consider at this point in your research.

Most of the major websites allow you to upload your ancestors' details into a tree. These include Ancestry, Find my Past, genesreunited.co.uk and familysearch.org. You have a choice whether or not to make your tree public. Those who have public trees allow other subscribers to see them. This can be very useful when you reach a dead end, but BE VERY CAREFUL. As I have stated before, it is not wise to just take other people's records at face value. Use them as a starting point to further your own research when you hit a brick wall, but ALWAYS CHECK THE INFORMATION OUT FOR YOURSELF.

You may find that by messaging others they will have proof that they can send you, but in my experience, it is often the case that they have just taken the information from someone else and have no idea of the original source.

One plus side to all of this is that you may find relatives that you never knew about. Whilst tracing my own family tree I found second and third cousins from Australia, Canada and other parts of the U.K., some of whom I have kept in contact with.

There is a downside though if you are not careful. When I started out, I spent many, many hours just copying out information from other people's trees. In retrospect it was mainly a complete waste of time for the reasons stated earlier.

If you choose not to add your own family tree to one of these sites, you can still view others' trees and, if you are a subscriber, you can contact them for further details.

You can also build your chart by buying or downloading one of the various tree-building software packages. I use Family Tree Maker, but there are others available.

Once you have traced the line back beyond 1921, then you can begin searching those all-important censuses...

CHAPTER 3

Censuses

About the Censuses

The first British census took place in 1801 during the reign of George III. At first it was more or less just a population count; no individual details being recorded.

In 1841, just after Queen Victoria came to the throne, the first more detailed census was taken. The facts that were recorded were their names, where they lived, their age (to within five years), their occupation, and whether or not they were born in the county that they then resided in.

From 1851 their exact age was recorded, also the town of their birth, their marital status, their relationship to the head of the house and whether they were blind, deaf or dumb.

You will almost certainly find that in some cases the age indicating the year of birth seems to vary from one census to the next. This could be for several reasons. Children's ages might be exaggerated to get around the Factory Acts or other child labour laws. Couples may have lied about their age to the authorities or each other. Or it could simply be that the person giving the information to the enumerator didn't know the exact age of their spouse or children.

Most entries regarding the relationship to the head of the household are straightforward, such as wife, son, daughter. Some are not so obvious. The term 'in-law' often referred to a 'step' relation and sometimes a brother-in-law or sister-in-law as we use the term today, was simply referred to as a brother or sister.

You will often see the terms boarder and lodger. Generally speaking, a boarder is a person who shares the dinner table with the family. A lodger is someone who has separate accommodation from the householder.

Subsequent censuses have included various amendments.

In 1871 another category was added, whether idiot, imbecile or lunatic (all perfectly acceptable medical terms at the time).

Officially an idiot was a person who had suffered with a mental disorder since birth. An imbecile is someone who had fallen in later life into a state of chronic dementia, and a lunatic was a mentally ill person who may have periods of lucidity. However, none of these guidelines were strictly adhered to and they often overlapped.

CENSUSES

From 1891 in Wales and 1901 on the Isle of Man, the language spoken was added.

In 1911 the length of marriage and the number of children to the married couple (and how many still surviving) were also included. It also gives the number of rooms in the house, giving a clearer indicator to the size of the dwelling.

At the time of writing, the 1921 census is only available to buy on Find My Past. A transcript costs £2.50 and an original image costs £3.50. There is a 10% discount for those with a 12-month subscription.

The census was taken on the 19th of June 1921 after being delayed by two months due to industrial unrest. There were thirty-eight million people in England and Wales at the time.

As well as all the information on the previous censuses, it also registered their place of work, employer details, and gave 'divorced' as an option for marital status, which was stated by 16,000 people, almost certainly less than the true number due to the stigma at the time.

Because of the vast number of casualties in World War I, there were 1,096 women for every 1,000 men recorded in the census, and far more women were employed.

For the purpose of this chapter, I will be referring to the censuses carried out in England and Wales. For other countries please see the relevant chapters.

These ten-yearly censuses have taken place ever since 1841 (apart from during the Second World War) and are available for the general public to view after a hundred years.

Unfortunately, there will be an exception in 2031, as the 1931 censuses for England and Wales were destroyed in a fire in 1942 where they were kept in storage in Hayes, Middlesex.

Ironically, this was not caused by any enemy bombs and the exact cause of the fire has never been established. It was concluded that it was probably caused by one of the fire watchers carelessly discarding a cigarette end!

This might have meant that there was a huge gap in records between 1921 and 1951.

However, there are records of households in 1939 available, because in September of that year at the outbreak of war, the government carried out a survey in order to access who needed identity cards and later ration cards. This Register includes the names, addresses and occupations of the population of England and Wales at the time, some forty-one million people. These records are available on Find my Past and Ancestry.

With regard to the ten-yearly censuses, schedules were handed out days before the allotted date to each household, and people were asked to complete the details of who was living in their house on the designated night. These details were then gathered by the enumerator who copied them into his book.

1911 is the only year where the original documents completed by the householders themselves still exist, so it is possible to see your ancestor's actual handwriting.

During the early years, only a small proportion of the population could read or write, so the enumerator would often have to take the information orally.

This accounts for a variety of errors, including the variations of spelling of names that we often find in different censuses. Compulsory education did not come into England until 1870 (and even this was often waivered in agricultural areas).

In the earlier censuses you will find the symbols / and //. The former denotes the end of a household and the latter the end of a dwelling. This is a good indication of how cramped conditions might have been for your ancestors.

You will often see Do. written. This simply means ditto. The entry above is the same word as this one. Other abbreviations are also used such as Ag. Lab. (Agricultural Labourer) and M.S. and F.S. (Male and Female Servants)

Obtaining the Censuses

To view the original censuses, you will need to subscribe to one of the websites that holds them online. (If you have the time and good access to your local library it is always worth checking with them because they often hold subscriptions to these websites and allow you to access them for free). Some County Archives also hold copies online or on microfilm and the National Archives at Kew allows free viewing. However, subscribing yourself means that you have access 24/7 and can therefore research in your own time and at your own pace.

The websites that hold copies of all the original records are Ancestry and Find my Past. On these sites it is possible to see the entries for yourself. This is especially useful if the writing is slightly illegible as errors in transcripts can occur.

I would just note here that familysearch.org, which is a free website, does offer transcripts of the censuses, so this is also an option if you just want information. However, as I have stated before, please bear in mind the possibility of human error whilst transcribing the documents. I always look at original documents if they are available.

There are other websites that offer subscriptions to view the censuses, but in my opinion, it is more economical to use sites that offer a lot of other useful documentation for your money.

There is more than one way to look up the information you need. On Ancestry the best way is to click on the census you require on the home page (always work backwards from the latest one) then put the following in the search facility that comes up: name (you have a choice of an exact name or variants), age (always add at least a couple of years either way in the additional box as ages are not always recorded exactly) and place of birth (click on the correct place name that comes up in the drop box after you begin typing).

CENSUSES

If it is a very common name (or you can't find it on the first search) then add additional facts such as the name of the spouse or parents. If you still have no luck then try omitting some of the search information, like where they were born. (County boundaries have changed over the years and sometimes this seems to confuse the situation).

On Ancestry there is another, although somewhat laborious way to find who you are looking for. I recommend this if all else fails. On the search button at the top, click on 'Census & Electoral Rolls' then where you have the option to 'Browse the Collections' complete the drop boxes until you get to the Civil Parish. It will then come up with a list of Enumeration Districts. If you are lucky there may be only one or two of these. If not, you may have a long search on your hands. Click on each district and then go through each page of the census, carefully looking for names that might be your ancestor, but have been incorrectly transcribed.

On Find my Past the search is similar, but here you need to begin on the home page by putting in the name, year of birth (again with an option to search a few years either way) and place of birth. This will take you to all options available for that information. Click on the 'Census, Land and Surveys' option in the box. This will bring up a list of all the relevant records, starting with a list of the first available census and continuing chronologically. You will need to scroll down these, clicking through the pages until you get to the year you are interested in.

If you cannot find what you are looking for then go to the 'Edit Search' option and tick the boxes under the names to allow variations in spelling. If you still have no luck, then remove the place of birth and perhaps add family members.

If after all this searching there is no trace of your ancestor, then move on. There are occasions, for whatever reason, that people were missed off the censuses. I have found this especially true in the 1841 records. The important thing is to find at least one census where the person whose name you know is a child, living with one or both parents. When you have this, you have a new name, a generation further back and the search can continue.

The one drawback to censuses is that because of reasons already explained, details in some of the censuses may not be totally accurate. As it was common for the information to be given by one member of the household, some facts might not be known. This is especially true if the person is a lodger or a visitor to the house rather than a family member. I am sure there were cases when any old information was given just to keep the enumerator happy.

Sometimes ages are inconsistent from one census to another. Perhaps an elderly relative is staying, and their exact age has been forgotten, or as mentioned before, perhaps a wife (or husband) has lied about their age to their spouse!

Places of birth are also variable. On one census a person might give the name of the actual hamlet they were born

CENSUSES

in, in another a nearby town and perhaps in a third, just the county. It is also worth bearing in mind that sometimes people would give their place of birth as the first town or village that they recall living in.

When these anomalies occur, it is always worth looking at the general picture. If there is one inconsistency and everything else ties in, then chances are you have the right person. If you are still not sure, try looking at other censuses. If the Joe Bloggs you are uncertain of is in another year's census where you have already found your relative, then he is obviously not who you are looking for.

As you find each census, download it to your computer or memory stick (or print it out if using a library or archive facility and don't have a computer at home). As I have already mentioned, it is vital to keep all the information neatly in folders online if possible, and as hard copies. It's amazing how easy it is to end up with a complete jumble of information very quickly, so organisation is the key.

One last thing to mention here (and it is a trap I find myself falling into even now) is to assume that if you have found the person in some censuses, but then can't find them in subsequent ones, that this person has died. However, when you look for a death record, you can find no trace. If that person is a woman, then consider the fact she may have remarried. This was very common back in the days before the Welfare State. If a woman was widowed with young children, finding someone to look after herself and her family would have been vital. It was often the case that widowed men would be the choice. She could look after his motherless children; he could bring home the bacon!

Adding to Your Research

Once you have completed your search of all the available censuses, you can add to your original research like this:

Grandfather – <u>John Smith</u>

John was born on the 5th of January 1904 at 15 Oakham Street, Brighton.

In 1911 he was living with his parents William and Mary and his siblings Thomas aged 3 and Jane aged 3 months at 22 Albert Square, Brighton.

John married Anne Thomas on the 12th of July 1928 in St Peter's Church, Brighton.

According to his marriage certificate John was a General Labourer.

On his daughter Jane's marriage certificate in 1968 it states he was a Factory Worker.

John died of chronic bronchitis on the 15th of December 1978 at 17 Factory Road, Brighton.

Great Grandfather – <u>William Smith</u>

William was born about 1872 in Brighton.

CENSUSES

In 1911 William was living with his wife Mary and his children James, Eliza, Maggie, Jane and John at 22 Albert Square, Brighton. He was a Coal Man.

The 1911 census has given you the information you need about William Smith, from here you can go back through the censuses and also find his birth, marriage and death in the GRO indexes, buying the certificates if needed (or wanted).

From here, for the next couple of generations, just continue in this way. When you reach a point where someone is born before 1837, then it's time to start exploring parish records...

CHAPTER 4

Birth, Marriage and Death – Part 2

How Were These Events Recorded Before 1837?

Prior to 1538 very few records were kept. Before the dissolution of the monasteries in 1535, the monks were the principal record keepers. These records, for the most part, would have been limited to Royalty and Gentry. So, these elite, along with notable artists, writers, inventors and the like whose lives may have been documented by historians, were the exception. For the clear majority of people who were serfs and peasants, no written record would have been required or considered necessary.

However, in 1538 Thomas Cromwell, Henry VIII's chief minister, ordered that every wedding, baptism and burial was to be recorded. Every parson, vicar or curate of the parish was to make entries of every christening, wedding and burial.

The parish had to provide a sure coffer with two locks, the parson having the custody of one key, the wardens the others. These entries were to be made each Sunday after service in the presence of one of the wardens. If these rules were not adhered to, a penalty of three shillings and fourpence was issued, to be used for the upkeep of the church. (This penalty was later changed by Edward VI in 1547 to be put in the poor box).

There may be some gaps in parish registers between 1553 and 1558 when the Catholic Mary Tudor was on the throne.

Most of the early records were recorded on paper, often loose sheets, but in 1597 under the reign of Elizabeth I, it was ordered that parchment books were to be used and the earlier records were to be transcribed onto parchment. Inevitably, some never were and have been lost. Also in 1597, a second copy of the records had to be made and sent to the bishop annually.

There may be more gaps in the records during the English Civil War and Commonwealth (1642–1660), as they were poorly kept or hidden, and again some have been lost.

Various amendments were added over the following years, relating to penalties and what was to be entered in the registers. In 1812 it was ordered that baptisms, marriages and burials were to be entered in separate, specially printed books, eight entries per page and including more information.

Non-Conformists were those who 'did not conform' – in other words, did not belong to the Church of England. These groups might be Protestants (including Presbyterians, Baptists, Methodists, Independents, Congregationalists and Quakers) or Roman Catholics.

Most people prior to 1837 were baptised, married and buried in the local Church of England parish, regardless of their beliefs. Even after the Toleration Act of 1689 granting the freedom to worship however one chose, many still registered these events in the local Parish Church. However, some Non-Conformist chapels and churches did keep their own registers.

For baptisms and burials these records continued to be the main source of record keeping until 1837, but for marriages it was a different story. Prior to the mid-eighteenth century, little attempt was made to control marriage. 'Contract marriages' were common among the protestant population. They believed that a marriage was binding without ceremony or rites so long as both parties agreed to the contract. This caused many problems as the agreement was unenforceable in law.

Clandestine marriages, or 'Fleet' marriages, so called because they occurred mainly near the Fleet River in London (although they took place in other locales, as well), were marriages performed by a clergyman, but usually in secret with false licences. In 1690 the government introduced a stamp tax on marriages to raise money, and these clandestine marriages meant a serious lack of potential income from the tax.

So in 1753, in an effort to regularise the solemnization of marriages, Hardwicke's Marriage Act was passed in England and Wales. It was effective from January 1754 and required that almost all couples had to be married in the Parish Church for the marriage to be deemed legal. Members of the Society of Friends (Quakers) and Jews were exempt from the Act and allowed to keep their own records.

The marriage was supposed to take place after banns had been called, in the home parish of one party, or else by licence. Banns are an official announcement of a marriage which is read out during the preceding weeks. This allows anyone who knows of a reason why the marriage shouldn't take place to speak up. The marriage licence had to be obtained from the Bishop of the Diocese, or from one of his surrogates, and there was a fee to be paid. Non-Conformist couples often married by licence, as this could be obtained quickly and eliminated the need for banns to be called for three successive Sundays in a Parish Church they never normally attended.

From 1836 marriages were allowed to take place in non-Conformist places of worship providing they had been licensed to perform marriage ceremonies.

Mostly the churches only recorded the religious ceremonies, i.e., baptisms, marriages and burials, so it isn't always possible to find exact dates of birth and death. However, whilst we can be pretty sure that there is not much time difference between death and burial; birth and baptism is not so straightforward. Babies were usually baptised whilst still infants, but occasionally, for whatever reason, some were baptised much later. Often their age is recorded on the baptism records if they are not babies, but not always. Also, it is sometimes only the father's name on the baptism records, so without a relevant marriage record, the trail can sometimes end there.

Marriage records can often reveal interesting information such as whether or not a person was literate. A cross by a name and the word 'mark' indicates that a person could not write. They can also tell us whether the individuals were widowed, and the man's occupation.

Burial records also occasionally have interesting little snippets of information, e.g., William Brown – Ancient man!

Occasionally records of males have the suffix Junior (Jnr) or Senior (Snr) added, which denotes that the father or son had the same first name, another useful piece of information.

Obtaining Parish Records

Chances are that the first record you will want to look up is a baptism. The censuses will have given you a rough idea of when and where the person you are looking for was born. Bear in mind that if you only have them in the 1841 census that ages were rounded up or down, so might be less accurate. Also, it only stated whether the person was born in the same county as where they then resided. As I have mentioned before, ages are often inaccurate in other censuses, so don't be too rigid in your search. This is also true of places.

My first port of call is usually Ancestry or Find my Past. Again, if you are not a subscriber, then familysearch.org and freereg.org.uk do supply transcripts, but again I would emphasise how transcripts can on occasion be inaccurate, but they are better than no information at all, and may even lead to clues as to where you may find them on the other sites.

If you are a subscriber to one of the websites, then log in and input as much information as you have into the search facilities. You have options of doing a general search which will show any information that tallies with the name and dates you have put in, or you can be more precise and just click on the birth, marriage and death sections and then even more specifically, the births. This is my preferred method because if you start finding other information at this stage it is easy to get things jumbled up and confused. I always try (although not always successfully), to be as methodical as I can.

If you have no luck finding a match at this stage, try being a bit broader in your search. Instead of putting in a town, put the county; give a little more leeway in the dates and check the box that allows for variants in spelling. Remember, names were often spelt differently in an age when not everyone could read. If an enumerator of the censuses was not familiar with the name, he might just write it down as he thought best, based on the spoken word of an illiterate family member.

On the other hand, if you find there are just too many possibilities, then try being more specific. If you have the marriage certificate, you should have the father's name so add that to your search. If they lived with their parents in the censuses then you will have both names, even better.

As you narrow it down, it is worth checking each possibility. It is often the case that children were named after their parents or grandparents, so look for other family member names on the censuses. However, never take this fact alone as evidence as there were far fewer forenames used than there are now, and some names were very common. Occasionally if there is a very unusual name, then this might be a more precise indicator that you are on the right track.

There are also other possibilities that might lead you to the information you seek. Useful sites that could be of help are genesreunited.co.uk (this requires a subscription), parishregister.co.uk and one of the Online Parish Clerk websites (a list of these can be found at ukbmd.org.uk/online_parish_clerk). This list is not exhaustive and new websites are springing up all the time, so it might be worth putting your ancestor's name in a search engine at this point, although unless it is a very unusual name, this is not very likely to help.

It may be that after all this you still have no luck, and your online search might end there. At this stage it is worth considering the possibility of finding a local family history group website or even visiting local archives. I will talk more about that later in the chapter.

However, if you do find what you are looking for (which is most often the case) then you will find one of two things. Either there will be a transcript of the document or, if you are lucky, the original images will be available. If you subscribe to both aforementioned sites and one only has the transcript, then look at the other. Different sites have different original document images, and they are adding to them all the time.

So, you now have a baptism (and possibly a birth) date. This will show at least the father's name and probably both parents' names, (or just the mother's if the birth was illegitimate). If you already knew these from the censuses, then it will confirm the research. If you didn't then it has added to the information and taken you back yet another generation.

Either way the next step is to find their marriage record. This is done in exactly the same way as finding the baptism (with different search options available). Likewise, if you want to find burial records use the same route. There are also websites such as findagrave.com, billiongraves.com and deceasedonline.com that may be useful here. These are particularly helpful if you want to locate a grave. Having said that, the majority of people were buried in unmarked or simple graves that have long since gone to seed and are therefore not still locatable.

It is useful to note that prior to the Industrial Revolution (and in some cases for some considerable time after it), most people lived, married and died in the same small village or were married to someone in an adjoining village. This makes tracing them much easier than it would be today. However, don't forget that parish boundaries also cross county borders, so if the parish you are looking for is close to a border, check out the next county as well.

If you are lucky, you may find that you can trace your ancestors back a long way, but unfortunately it is often the case that you meet a stumbling block or dead end along the way. If there is more than one possibility that the records you find belong to your ancestor, then don't guess. Best to just make a note of the possibilities and end there. Perhaps at some point, some clue will arise as to which record is correct and then you can move on safe in the knowledge that you are once again on the right track.

Once you have exhausted all genealogy website options then it is time to check out the local family history group sites. As I have stated before, it is always best to email or ring them first to see exactly what they can offer. Some (although few) will do a limited search for you for free, but most will charge a small subscription fee. Always check what you will get for your money. Sometimes they only offer services to people in person, but mostly they are broader in their approach, and it is worth the fee. I have found that by joining some of these societies, I have been put in touch with other useful resources like local libraries and I even found people, who for a much smaller fee than the local archives charge, are willing to look up records on your behalf.

The final ports of call are the local archives themselves. If you can get to them then they are well worth a visit. Always check out what is available first. Make a list of everything you want to find (it's often best to wait until you have a few blanks in your tree to optimise your journey), then book an appointment. You will probably have to become a member which you should be able to do online, then you will need to take some ID with you, to confirm who you are. Local archives hold all available records, so if you draw a blank here then you can be pretty certain that unless somewhere out there someone owns a dusty old bible with the generations recorded in it, that you have come to the end of the road.

Accept it and move on to the next surname. That is a whole new journey!

What do Parish Records Look Like?

This varies a great deal, but an example is shown on here:

[Handwritten parish record of Baptisms in 1777, listing entries including Edward Gadd, John Dorset, Polly Sharp, Ann Dale, Sarah Martha Leifchild, Ann Quenton, James Knowlton, John Gates, Elizabeth Coles, Robert Emerton, Charles Walker, Mary Ann Richardson, Mary Jones, and Joseph Lawford, with baptism dates from February through July 1777.]

Adding to Your Research

Let's update our hypothetical William Smith:

> Great Grandfather – William Smith
>
> William was born on the 11th of November 1871 at 17 Marine View, Brighton.
>
> He was illegitimate.
>
> In 1881 he was living with his grandmother Eliza, mother

BIRTH, MARRIAGE AND DEATH – PART 2

Margaret, Aunt Fanny and Uncle Benjamin at 19 Marine View, Brighton.

William married Mary Holmes on the 12th of July 1890 at Brighton Register Office.

At the time of his marriage, he was living at 6 Claremont Row, Brighton and was a General Labourer.

In 1891 he was living with his wife and new baby James at 14 Newhaven Street, Brighton. He was a General Labourer.

In 1901 he was living with his wife and children James 10, Eliza 7, Maggie 5 and Jane 2 at 60 Carlton Hill, Brighton. He was a Coal Merchant.

In 1904 on his son John's birth certificate, William was living at 15 Oakham Street, Brighton.

In 1911 he was living with his wife Mary and his children James, Eliza, Maggie, Jane and John at 22 Albert Square, Brighton. He was a Coal Man.

William died on the 25th of September 1943 of carcinoma of the bladder at 31 Sussex Terrace, Brighton.

His daughter Eliza of 37 Sussex Terrace was present at his death.

Great x 2 Grandmother – <u>Margaret Smith</u>

Margaret was born in the first quarter of 1849 at 17 Crescent Cottages, Brighton.

In 1851 she was living with her parents and siblings at 28 Chapel Street, Brighton.

In 1861 she was living with her parents and siblings at 20 Marine View, Brighton.

In 1871 she was living with her mother Eliza, son William, sister Fanny and brother Benjamin at 19 Marine View, Brighton. (Between then and 1881, according to the next census, this property fell down!)

She was a Dressmaker.

There is no trace of Margaret in the 1881 census. In 1891 she was living with George Mason as his housekeeper at 3 Claremont Row, Brighton. In 1901 she was living with George Mason as his housekeeper at 20 Woburn Place, Brighton.

Her occupation was given as Charwoman.

In 1911 she was living with her niece Ellen Johnson (her sister Fanny's daughter), Ellen's husband Henry, his brother George and Ellen's illegitimate son Richard at 28 Sycamore Place, Brighton.

Margaret never married.

She died on the 9th of May 1922 at 250, Elm Grove, Brighton (The Workhouse & Infirmary) of carcinoma uteri and cardiac failure.

At the time of her death, she had been living with her sister Fanny at 37 Hardy Terrace, Brighton. She was listed as a Charwoman and Spinster.

Margaret was probably illiterate, at least at the time of William's birth, as only her 'mark' not her signature was on the birth certificate.

Great x 3 Grandfather – <u>Jonathan known as John.</u>

Jonathan was born on the 3rd of February 1810 in Chipping Barnet, Hertfordshire.

He was baptised on the 4th of March 1810 in Chipping Barnet and again on the 4th June 1812 at Jireh Chapel, Cliffe, Lewes.

Jonathan married Eliza Hurst on the 26th of March 1837 in St. Andrews Church, Hove.

In 1841 he was living with wife and children James 3 and Fanny 1 in Essex Street, Brighton.

In 1851 he was living with his wife and children James 13, Fanny 11, Esther 9, Jonathan 7, Thomas 4 and Margaret 2 at 28 Chapel Street, Brighton.

His occupation was a Painter.

In 1861 he was living with his wife and children Esther 18, Thomas 13, Margaret 11 and Benjamin 7 at 20 Marine View, Brighton.

He was still a Painter.

Jonathan died on the 24th of March 1866 at 18 Marine View, Brighton, Sussex of paralysis/cerebral effusion (brain haemorrhage).

Great x 4 Grandfather – <u>William Smith</u>

William was probably baptised on the 14th of August 1777 in Chipping Barnet, Hertfordshire. *

He married Esther Wilkins on the 14th September 1807 at St Clement Danes, Westminster.

William was a widower when he married Esther.

In 1841 he was living with his wife at 17 St John's Street, New Shoreham

He was a Railway Worker.

William died on the 19th of June 1847 at Nelson Place, Brighton of Old Age.

*This is probably William because we know that his son Jonathan was baptised in Chipping Barnet. However, as we only have him in the 1841 census which gives no positive place of birth (other than it was not in Sussex), and as William Smith is such a common name, we can go no further at present.

By now you should be well on the way to having a good idea about at least one branch of your family tree. It's great knowing the names and abodes of your forefathers, but research becomes much more exciting when you begin to incorporate other factors.

You may already have learned something from the censuses and birth, marriage and death records such as their occupations. Also, you may have stumbled across some other information whilst doing those previous checks. Sometimes when you put a name into a search box on the websites, it leads you to other information about the person. When this happens, I try not to let it distract me from the main name search, but I don't always succeed and find myself heading down another path, which can side-track me for a while.

My advice is, whenever possible, don't let yourself be distracted. Make a note of anything you think may prove to be useful and return to it later. Keep to the task in hand, it really does save confusion.

Whether or not you have come across other information, now is the time to begin thinking about it...

CHAPTER 5

The Class System and Occupations

Early Forms of Society in England

At the top of Celtic society was the king or chieftain. Below him were the craftsmen, then farmers. There was also a class of slaves. However, the Celts had no political union amongst them, just a good deal of fighting.

When the Romans came to our shores, the higher members of society took on the Roman way of life, living in villas with luxuries such as windows and art. For the lower classes though life stayed much the same. They dwelt in simple huts and lived off the land. There were still slaves, who were simply the property of the rich.

When the Roman's left, the standard of living took a backward turn.

THE CLASS SYSTEM AND OCCUPATIONS

At the pinnacle of Anglo-Saxon society were the thanes who enjoyed hunting and feasting, but they lived in large, crowded halls with no panes of glass and no chimneys. Below them were the churls who mainly rented land from the thanes.

Some churls were rich, others were poor, but at the very bottom of society were the class of slaves known as thralls. For them life was very hard.

Until 1066 this primitive feudal system was evolving slowly with the emergence of small towns, but when William the Conqueror took over, he introduced a new system. They were a race of tribes and their new king claimed all the land in England and divided the land between himself (about twenty per cent), the Church (about twenty-five per cent) and the remainder was given to Norman soldiers and nobles who had helped him conquer the country. All the land was still owned by the king, but the nobles or barons occupied and ruled over their own manor in exchange for providing services for him.

WILLIAM the CONQUEROR.

A manor consisted of a manor house, one or more villages, and land which consisted of meadows, pasture, woodland, and cultivated fields. The fields were divided into strips; one third for the lord of the manor, less for the church, and the remainder for the peasants. For the villagers at least half of the week was spent maintaining land belonging to the lord and the church. The rest of the time the villagers were free to work their own land.

The feudal system was based on a social hierarchy. At the summit was the king, followed by the barons. The knights or vassals came next. They leased land from the barons and in return, they provided military service to the king at the time of need and protected the baron and his family.

At the bottom of the chain were the peasants, also known as villeins or serfs. They were granted land by the knights, but they had to provide food and service to the higher classes on demand. They had no rights, and they were also not allowed to marry without permission from their lords. They were not allowed to leave the manor.

During the 12th and 13th centuries with the expansion of trade, money rather than land ownership began to move society away from the feudal system. A new class of merchants trading in all sorts of goods sprang up, and serfs began to utilise this trade and pay for their farms with money rather than services. This led to the rise of the tenant farmer. By the end of the Middle Ages, many serfs were able to purchase their freedom and most feudal lords had become landlords. Knights began to be replaced by large mercenary armies.

Even though feudal land tenure was not actually abolished in England until 1660, by the end of the 14th century many of the changes which were to result in the Renaissance in the following century, had taken place. However, the nobility did not disappear, they merely continued on as aristocracy.

THE CLASS SYSTEM AND OCCUPATIONS

The hierarchy now consisted of the aristocracy at the top, followed by the gentry (gentlemen who owned substantial amounts of land and usually had a coat of arms). Alongside them were the merchants who gained wealth in industries like wool processing, shipbuilding and banking. Below them were the yeomen who owned their own land and leased it to tenant farmers, also tradesmen who were crafts workers and shopkeepers. Tenant farmers or husbandmen followed, and right at the bottom were the unskilled workers.

In the 16th century half of the population lived at a basic subsistence level, which gave them enough food, shelter and clothes to survive. Humanist ideals were beginning to emerge, but the poor unskilled workers, particularly in rural areas in times of hardship, would still sometimes starve.

In 1577 a church minister named William Harrison wrote in his work "A Description of England":

> "We in England divide our people commonly into four sorts – gentlemen, citizens, yeomen, and labourers. First there are the gentlemen. After the King, the chief gentlemen are the prince, dukes, marquises, earls, viscounts and barons. These are called lords and noblemen. Next are knights, esquires and last of all those who are simply called gentlemen."

The latter probably included the merchants.

Harrison goes on to describe citizens as those who lived in cities and did important jobs. The yeomen, he declared, owned a certain amount of land and were 'well off'. Finally, he described labourers and craftspeople as poor farm workers, tailors, shoemakers, carpenters, bricklayers and so on. He also added:

"As for slaves, we have none".

However, despite the continuing hierarchy, for the first time, social mobility became possible. With hard work and luck, a farmer could become a yeoman. A yeoman could buy a coat of arms and become a gentleman. This could cost more than £100 (at a time when a decent house could be bought for £60), so it was by no means a possibility for all. Also, a rich merchant might marry into the gentry or nobility. It was possible for an ambitious young man to rise in the world.

But for the majority, the simple peasant labourers, their lot was unlikely to change. Their crucial, but humble role in society was, in part, reinforced by the Church. The belief was that God had created a 'Grand Chain' where every man played his part. Just as the King was there by Divine Right, so it was that those at the very bottom of society were there because it was God's will. To rebel against this could have consequences in the afterlife, so very few would have risked eternal damnation by attempting to change things.

During the 18th century, the number of yeomen declined and the gap between the top and the bottom of society was larger.

However, whilst their income and comforts may have been radically opposed, the 18th century artist William Hogarth saw similarities and depicted both ends of society as "Gin Lane" and "Midnight Modern Conversation":

THE CLASS SYSTEM AND OCCUPATIONS

Victorian Society

In Victorian Society there were several layers to what had become known as the working classes. Three out of four people did manual labour. The majority worked on the land, in domestic service and in factories as well as other manual trades such as building and mining. These labourers lived hand to mouth, so in times of sickness and as they grew older and less physically able, they might need to rely on charity or at worst would be forced to enter the workhouse.

Right at the bottom of the social ladder was a form of underclass which consisted of petty criminals, prostitutes and chancers, commonly frequenters of gin houses; they were often homeless and destitute. However, most of the lower classes were hard working and on the right side of the law, and could for the most part, keep a roof over their head.

THE CLASS SYSTEM AND OCCUPATIONS

Within the family, when the children were very small, the wife would not be able to go out to work. She may do some form of paid labour at home or take in lodgers, but usually the family would have been very poor. This meant as soon as the children were old enough, they were sent out to work and the family's income would temporarily increase.

The 1833 Factory Act stated that children under nine were not allowed to work, those up to thirteen could work no more than nine hours a day and those up to eighteen no more than twelve hours. They were also not allowed to work at night. This of course was not always enforced, and young children were still employed in what we would consider arduous conditions, in order for the families to survive.

However, eventually the children would leave and start their own families and the parents were left alone as they were becoming feebler and less able to work, so once again their standard of living would decrease.

Most people would probably have merely accepted this. Social mobility, although becoming increasingly more possible, was still rare. The working classes were born, worked and died in the same village or town with no prospect of improving their lot.

The image below from Punch Magazine in 1856 shows crossing-sweepers. Children who would sweep aside horse manure so those of the wealthier classes could cross the street without getting dirty.

THE CROSSING-SWEEPER NUISANCE.

Slightly above the unskilled and semi-skilled labourers, although still considered working class, were the skilled craftsmen and artisans such as blacksmiths, tailors and millers.

The 1851 census showed there to be upwards of one and a half million agricultural workers in Britain. By 1867 this number had dwindled to below one million and unskilled factory workers and domestic servants were ever increasing in number. Those who worked on the land were almost always the lowest paid, with their average wage being about fourteen shillings a week. However, they would have had an advantage over the town workers, who would not usually have had access to any land where they could grow or forage for food to subsidise their income. Factory workers may have earned as much as twenty-two shillings a week, whilst the aforementioned craftsmen could have expected to make on average twenty-five to thirty-five shillings.

THE CLASS SYSTEM AND OCCUPATIONS

After the working classes came the new breed of middle classes. They made up about fifteen per cent of the population. This group of people were diverse and included everyone from bankers, lawyers, doctors and the clergy as well as the lesser paid clerks (who might earn half the pay of a manual labour), because income was not necessarily a factor. It was more a case of education. To be a clerk or a shopkeeper you didn't need a formal education, but you did need to be literate, something unnecessary for the lower-class occupations.

The middle classes for the most part, consisted of hard-working, church-going individuals who resented the idleness of the aristocracy and looked down on the working classes, who they considered to be less sober, pious and industrious than themselves. They valued education and aimed to send their children to private schools or one of the Grammar Schools that were now springing up.

Still right at the top was the elite class of land-owning aristocrats and the gentry. Aristocrats (men who carried a hereditary title) could make up to £30,000 a year (compare that with an agricultural worker's £25 a year) from their land. They were expected to sit in Parliament and subsequently spent half their time in London.

The landed gentry often known as Squires were educated well-bred men who spent most of their time on their estate taking an active interest in local issues.

As the Industrial Revolution progressed and more and more people moved from the countryside to the town, the need for better working conditions increased. Trade Unions began to emerge and with the rights for the working man finally being recognised, the elite classes could no longer afford to exploit their labouring employees. The middle classes began to have more influence and with much more chance of upward mobility, the class system became more blurred. By the end of the 20th century there was still the basic Victorian three class system, but the lower classes no longer lived on the breadline. The Welfare State and the NHS contributed to equality in health and social care. However, a byproduct of this Utopian ideal was the emergence of a new underclass. No longer the poverty stricken, but those who sometimes used the 'system' to their own advantage.

One last thing worth a mention here is the inequality between the genders. Until 1870, when a woman married, all her property became her husband's and despite getting the vote at the age of thirty in 1918, it was not until 1928 that the age was lowered to twenty-one to coincide with men.

Obtaining Records that Give Clues to Your Ancestor's Occupation and Social Class

By now you will know many of your ancestors' occupations from the censuses and birth, marriage and death certificates. Occasionally you might be lucky enough to come across an occupation on older parish records if those who recorded them were more thorough in their work. However, there are other sources which may give you clues online.

THE CLASS SYSTEM AND OCCUPATIONS

On Ancestry in the Schools, Directories & Church Histories section you may find publications such as the Kelly's Directories which list the occupations of tradesmen, farmers, shopkeepers etc. Kelly's and other directories that can be found on Ancestry can be very useful because they can bridge the gap between censuses. Also, of course they are available for some time after the censuses.

On this subject, I was recently able to solve an ongoing family dispute for one of my clients. It was known that her great grandfather had been a publican for a while, but there was a difference of opinion between members of the family as to what pub he ran and in what village. From the 1901 census it was easy to conclude that one side of the argument was correct. However, I was also able to find an entry in Kelly's in 1899 which showed that at that time he was the landlord of the other pub in the other village, so it turned out that everyone was appeased!

Of course, these directories are not available yet for all counties, but additional information is being uploaded all the time, so as I have mentioned before it is always good to retrace your research every now and then. Also, keep checking for what is new on the websites and opt to have emails sent when new information becomes available.

Like Ancestry, Find my Past has a wealth of useful directories, as well as transcripts of London Apprenticeship Abstracts from 1442–1850. As many young men were sent to London to be apprenticed at their trade, this can be a very useful resource for the early centuries.

Other records such as Wills, Probates and Tax Records are all possible sources that may give a person's occupation.

Last Wills and Testaments can be particularly useful. Of course, they were only made by those who had money or property to leave behind, so they were certainly not drawn up for the majority. However, if you do have an ancestor who was a person of means, then they are sometimes a treasure trove of information. Many go back a long way, and the wording can be quite hard to decipher (see below). With a little practice and patience though you should find that you can at least get the gist of what is written. More than anything, I have found that Wills confirm information already gleaned. As well as occupations, it may give the names of the spouse and children and place of residence etc. This can be a blessing if you are a little uncertain of some of your facts.

Both Ancestry and Find My Past have many original documents and transcripts of Will and Probate records of varying collections and again the National Archives website may be of help.

How did Your Ancestor's Occupation fit in to the Social Hierarchy?

There are far too many occupations and variables to list them all here, but there are several good websites which give an idea of what your ancestor's standard of living might have been like. This list is certainly not exhaustive, but it includes:

www.bl.uk/victorian-britain

www.bbc.co.uk/history/british/victorians

www.logicmgmt.com

www.census1891.com

www.worldthroughthelens.com

www.victorianweb.org

CHAPTER 6

The Military

The Royal Navy

The Royal Navy was officially formed in 1660 after the restoration of King Charles II. However, there had been a naval force, albeit in times of conflict in England, for at least a thousand years previous to that. By the end of the 17th century, the Navy had grown into a considerable force due to the continuing wars in Europe. As the United Kingdom began to expand its Empire, the Royal Navy became the biggest maritime force in the world and indeed, is still the second biggest force in NATO.

Up until the early years of the 19th century, particularly in times of war, a common method of obtaining men for the Navy was the press gang or impressment as it was known. This was perfectly legal. Able men, often from the merchant navy, but also ordinary labourers and apprentices were taken by force and made to serve their country.

The British Army

It is often considered that the Restoration of 1660 also saw the birth of our modern British Army. However, fifteen years prior to that, Oliver Cromwell had set up his New Model Army which was the first time that a full-time professional militia had been formed within the three kingdoms of England, Ireland and Scotland. They proved to be a considerable force, but after the Restoration they were disbanded, and on 26th January 1661, Charles II issued the Royal Warrant that created the first regiments of what was to become the British Army.

The structure of this army has remained relatively unchanged to this day.

The Cavalry were troops who used horses, later replaced by tanks after the carnage of the First World War. The Artillery is trained to use heavy guns. The Engineers provide support

"The Battle of Waterloo" by Jan Willem Pieneman, 1824

for front line troops by carrying out and maintaining essential work such as bridge building. Finally, and historically the most common was the Infantry – foot soldiers who are the front-line attack in a conflict.

During the 18th century the public were wary of the amount of power the government held if in control of a large army, so in times of peace the numbers were kept to a minimum. When extra men were needed, they were raised by voluntary means or if that failed, by force. Several Recruiting Acts were passed which gave magistrates the right to press unemployed, but otherwise able-bodied men into service. These Acts also gave financial incentives to encourage enlistment. In 1757 this sum was £3, the equivalent of about two month's wages for a working-class man.

The Royal Air Force

The first powered airplane took to the skies on 17th December 1903 piloted by Orville Wright.

In 1912 the British government realised the potential of using aircraft in military situations and the Royal Flying Corps was formed as a part of the British Army. By the end of 1912, its aircraft consisted of twelve balloons and thirty-six airplanes. At the outbreak of the First World War in August 1914, the RFC went to France with just sixty-three airplanes. Its main task was aerial reconnaissance, but it soon became clear that it could play a much larger role. By 1918 it had over three thousand aircraft in action.

THE MILITARY

In 1910 the Royal Navy acquired its first aircraft, and in 1914 the Royal Naval Air Service was formed. It was mainly used to defend the home territories.

On the 1st of April 1918, The Royal Air Force came into being by merging the Royal Flying Corps and the Royal Naval Air Service. By the end of the War on the 11th November 1918 just seven months after its formation, the RAF had become the most powerful air force in the world with over twenty-two thousand aircraft and more than two hundred and ninety thousand officers and men. All this in fewer than fifteen years since Orville Wright first took to the skies!

A First World War Recruitment Poster

The ranks of all three branches of the armed forces can be confusing and some ranks such as Warrant Officer and Corporal have been added over time. On the next page is a rough guide comparing equivalent ranks to help you ascertain how high up your ancestor was in the pecking order. In some cases, there may not be direct equivalents, but you should get an idea.

GROW YOUR OWN FAMILY TREE

ARMY	ROYAL AIR FORCE	ROYAL NAVY
Field Marshall	Marshall of the Royal Air Force	Admiral of the Fleet
General	Air Chief Marshall	Admiral
Lieutenant-General	Air Marshall	Vice Admiral
Major General	Air Vice-Marshall	Rear Admiral
Brigadier	Air Commodore	Commodore
Colonel	Group Captain	Captain
Lieutenant-Colonel	Wing Commander	Commander
Major	Squadron Leader	Lieutenant-Commander
Captain	Flight-Lieutenant	Lieutenant
Lieutenant	Flying Officer	—
—	—	Sub-Lieutenant
Second Lieutenant	Pilot Officer	—
—	—	Midshipman
Warrant Officer Class 1	Warrant Officer	Warrant Officer
Warrant Officer Class 2	—	—
Staff Sergeant	Flight-Sergeant/Chief Technician	Chief Petty Officer
Sergeant	Sergeant	Petty Officer
Corporal	Corporal	Leading Seaman
Lance Corporal	—	—
—	Junior Technician/Senior Aircraftman/Leading Aircraftman	Able Seaman
Private	Aircraftman	Ordinary Seaman

THE MILITARY

Obtaining Military Records

Often, one of the first things that crops up, is "What did my father/grandfather/great grandfather do in the First World War?"

Unfortunately, over half of the service records from this time were destroyed during the Blitz, but many do remain.

If the person that you are searching for was killed during action, then the best place to visit online is the Commonwealth War Graves Commission (cwgc.org). The records here are free to search.

If however, they survived, and you believe that they served in the British Army, then once again it is time to visit Ancestry and/or Find my Past. If you have been using these websites, then by now you should be familiar with the varying search facilities. Just use the drop boxes or sidebar searches to access what you are interested in.

These sites hold many of the surviving military records and are a reliable source, as they have images of the original handwritten documents. They can tell you when the person joined up, where they were stationed, if they were hospitalised, whether they had good conduct, when they were discharged from the services and whether they were awarded any medals.

A useful source for Royal Naval records, if you hold a subscription, is Find my Past. If not, then www.

nationalarchives.gov.uk might be useful. These records will confirm date and place of birth and the sailor's rank and number. The search is free, but if you want further information, you can download the original images for a small fee. If you visit the National Archives at Kew you will be able to search for the documents without charge.

Air force records are to be found on Find my Past and www.nationalarchives.gov.uk.

A further excellent source for all military records is fold3.com. Although it is a part of Ancestry, it holds records that ancestry.com does not, and you will sometimes be directed there when searching on Ancestry. Like most websites you can register for a free trial, but if you want more information later on, there is a subscription.

If you are content with just a short transcript to confirm that your relative was in the forces, then a visit to familysearch.org will probably be enough.

If all else fails and you happen to know the service number, then it might be worth checking forces-war-records.co.uk. As the transcripts only bring up a surname and an initial, without the service number it is not much help. This site is free to search, but if you find what you are looking for, then you will have to pay to view the transcript.

As well as the First World War, there are many other military records available on the previously mentioned websites. The censuses would have shown up any military personnel, so if this is the case then searching may well bring up the relevant documents relating to them. There are various records obtainable covering many conflicts, including the Crimean, Boer and even the Napoleonic Wars.

CHAPTER 7

Crime in the 18th and 19th Centuries

A Brief History of Crime in Victorian England

In the late 18th century and well into the 19th most of England only had unpaid Parish Constables to keep the peace in their town or village.

The first professional police force was founded in London in 1749 by Henry Fielding and consisted of six or seven respectable men who were paid to prevent and detect crime. They carried truncheons, handcuffs and pistols and came to be known as the Bow Street Runners.

In 1798 the River Police were set up in London to deter the huge amount of criminal activity associated with the stealing of goods from merchant ships. This was a cleverly organised system operating between sailors and men on the shore.

The River Police also carried pistols!

The Metropolitan Police force was established in 1829 by Robert Peel.

These 'Bobbies' or 'Peelers' as they became known had, for the first time, a uniform and were paid sixteen shillings a week. Initially the force consisted of a thousand men but steadily grew. The Bow Street Runners and the River Police were incorporated into the new force and gained a uniform but had to give up their pistols!

In 1851 the census identified thirteen thousand criminals in London. The proportion of criminals had probably not changed much over time, but with more crime detected and more access to newspapers, 'respectable' Londoners became more aware and more afraid of the lower classes.

Many boroughs and counties outside London began to employ their own police forces. They were still locally organised, because of the in-built English resistance to the idea of a central force such as existed on the Continent, but in 1862 the government finally decreed that every town should have its own force.

The way in which criminals were perceived evolved over the 19th century. In the beginning there was an idea of the working-class criminal at the bottom of society who was work shy, drunken, lazy and immoral. By the middle of the century, this had formulated into the notion of a 'criminal class', those that dwelt in the slums and hovels of the inner cities. By the end of the century with the new vogue of psychiatry, much more emphasis was put on the idea that criminals had an abnormal behaviour pattern, brought about by either nurture or nature.

George Cruikshank's original drawing of the young pickpocket Artful Dodger with Oliver Twist looking on

This meant that the way in which criminals were treated changed over time. At the beginning of the century, it was still not uncommon for people to be hanged for what we today would consider petty crimes, (public hangings went on until 1868), but by the time Queen Victoria came to the throne, the only crimes punishable by death were murder and treason. By then transportation had become a common choice of punishment.

This had been going on since the early 18th century when convicts were sent to North America, but ceased when America gained her independence in 1776. From then on Australia was their destination. Between 1787 and 1868 an estimated one hundred and sixty thousand men, women and children were sent halfway around the world to serve their sentence. Most never returned as, although they were free to come back to England after their sentence ended, their passage was not paid, and so the cost would have been out of reach for the majority.

Ironically, many ex-convicts who stayed in Australia went on to prosper, and they and their families probably fared much better in the long run than if they had spent their time in a prison cell in England.

Prisons changed dramatically from the 18th century onwards. Initially they had developed into overcrowded 'dens of iniquity' where criminals were placed just to get them off the streets. They had easy access to alcohol and paid their gaolers, so the better off had a better deal.

From the 1830s onwards new, larger prisons were built with the idea that prisoners should endure punishment. This punishment was generally pointless labour. One example was that inmates had to turn a crank ten thousand times during an eight-hour day. Officers could tighten the screws on the handles to make it harder – hence the slang term for prison officers – 'screws'.

By the 1860s prison reformers encouraged the idea that an attempt at reform was better than mere punishment, and more constructive labour such as farming and mailbag sewing was introduced. This took a while to catch on everywhere, but by the end of Victoria's reign in 1901, catching and punishing criminals had undergone an overwhelming change for the better.

Obtaining Criminal Records

To find out if anyone you are researching was ever charged with a criminal offence, the best source is (surprise, surprise!) Ancestry or Find my Past.

Ancestry holds the England & Wales Criminal Registers from 1791 to 1892. These registers provide information about the charged individual, their trial and sentence (if convicted) or another outcome. Information listed may include: the name, age, birthplace, crime, when and where tried, sentence (death, transportation, imprisonment, acquittal, etc.), where and when received and the date of execution or release.

Other records on this site include a calendar of prisoners, court records, warrants, pardons and transportation records as well as UK Police Gazettes between 1812 and 1927, which contain printed publications used for communication between members of the police force.

Find my Past also offers images of many original documents for England & Wales from 1770 to 1935. These documents may give you a physical description (height, complexion, build, visage, eyes, hair), character description, marital status, offence, plea, sentence, name of magistrate or judge, previous convictions, petitions for pardons and more.

Again, local archives may also hold relevant records that are not yet available online. If you know that your ancestor committed a crime and the date on which he was tried, it is well worth searching through the old newspapers which most archives hold.

Find my Past also has images of many newspaper records. Simply type in a name and use the filters such as place and time to narrow down your search.

Ancestry is linked to newspapers.com which also has British newspaper articles. A free 7-day trial is available.

Often using all of the available resources can complete the picture. I found the story of my ancestor (the wonderfully named Cephas Tree previously mentioned in Chapter 1) and his run-in with the law. Using the two websites and then travelling to the Keep (the East Sussex archive), I was able to get original images of his burglary conviction for which he was sentenced to hang along with his daughter Mary! I then found images of the reduction in their sentences to transportation, then Cephas' final pardon.

At the archives I found some wonderful newspaper reports.

According to the Brighton Herald 21st March 1807, when the guilty verdict and death sentence was announced "Mary Tree, pierced with horror, convulsed and screaming, was borne from the court".

Mary was transported to New South Wales on the Speke which set off in March 1808. She settled there and hopefully lived happily ever after. Cephas spent the rest of his life in his hometown of Brighton and died in 1816 at the age of seventy.

Another of my Brighton Ancestors, Esther Orchard was convicted of larceny in 1845, but I don't think I come from a particularly 'criminal class'. When all considered, for those hailing from the working classes in Victorian Britain with all its poverty, it is not surprising that the temptation to steal was often too strong to resist.

CHAPTER 8

The Poor Laws and the Workhouse

It is quite likely whilst you are doing your research that you will come across someone who, for one reason or another, had a stint in the workhouse.

The word 'workhouse' implies that the sole purpose of the institution was to give people employment. However, the workhouse was more than that. It provided an infirmary for those that couldn't work and often acted as a temporary refuge for those in need.

An example of this was my own grandfather who was born in the Brighton workhouse in 1888. He was illegitimate, and it is likely either that his mother was rejected by her family or that there was some kind of medical problem that required more than a midwife.

His mother, my great grandmother, was also illegitimate, and her mother never married nor had any more children. It fell upon her to bring up my grandfather (her grandson) whilst his mother got married (presumably not to his father) and went on to have eight more children. She lived just a few streets away.

The stigma of illegitimacy was such that it was rare for men to take on a child that was not their own, born out of wedlock. Perhaps that is why my great-great grandmother never married. I like to think that her love for her daughter was more important than her need for a man. Of course, this is probably just wishful thinking, something that you will find yourself doing a lot during your research!

Early Poor Law

Before the 14th century giving help to the poor was based on a purely voluntary, charitable basis. However, as is often the case with human nature, this could be taken advantage of. Able-bodied men could and would become beggars.

After the Black Death in 1349 there was a shortage of labour which forced up wages and meant some land went unused. The consensus amongst the landowners was that all able-bodied men should work. This led to the Statute of Labourers in 1351 which stated that all men who were able should work, and it made it illegal for anyone to give aid to able-bodied beggars.

In 1388 the Statute of Cambridge was passed that made each Hundred (an old administrative unit within a county) responsible for its own labourers and the infirmed.

These Acts were followed over the next two centuries by many others. The Vagabonds and Beggars Act of 1495 stated that:

> "Vagabonds, idle and suspected persons shall be set in the stocks for three days and three nights and have none other sustenance but bread and water and then shall be put out of Town. Every beggar suitable to work shall resort to the Hundred where he last dwelled, is best known, or was born and there remain upon the pain aforesaid."

The 1531 Vagabonds Act allowed for designated areas to beg, but this was usually limited to the infirmed. Any begging outside of these areas incurred harsh penalties.

In 1547 the Statute of Legal Settlement stated that an able-bodied beggar could be enslaved. However, it also decreed that houses should be built for the impotent poor, those too sick or elderly to work, and that they should be relieved or cured.

In 1572 after a trial run in several cities, the poor rate was introduced and administered by overseers who determined how the money was spent and to whom it was given.

In 1597 the Act for the Relief of the Poor was passed requiring all parishes to appoint an overseer who was responsible for finding work for those capable and looking after those who weren't.

It is interesting that the money raised by the poor rates was based (as is still the case with Council Tax) on the value of someone's property. As now, this was not the responsibility of the owner of the property, but the tenant. Hefty fines and even prison could result in failure to pay these rates. How little some things change!

The next big amendment was the Settlement Act of 1662. The rules for 'settlement' had their roots in the long-established laws of the 14th century. A man or unmarried woman's place of settlement was that of their father. If the child was illegitimate, then it was the place of their birth. This led to many unmarried pregnant women being taken to another parish just before the child was born. A married woman's place of settlement was that of her husband.

If work was scarce and a man wanted to seek work outside of his parish, he required a document which stated that should he not be able to support himself and his family in his new place of residence, then they were entitled to send him back to his place of settlement.

In 1697 an Act was passed requiring those who begged to wear a 'badge' of red or blue cloth on the right shoulder with an embroidered letter 'P' and the initial of their parish. This was rarely enforced and didn't last long.

Later Acts allowed for other ways to obtain settlement. Apprentices (some as young as seven), could claim their place of apprenticeship. Labourers who had worked continually for a year in one place could also claim settlement. Often contracts were given for three hundred and sixty-four days and sometimes labourers who were not happy in their new place of work would make sure they moved on before the year was up.

These settlement laws were amended many times in the subsequent centuries and were not finally abolished until 1948!

Below is a copy of my great-great great grandfather's settlement certificate. He was a ropemaker and set off to Hastings to find work. His son Cephas (you may remember him from Chapter 7) was the one set to commit burglary in his later life.

The New Poor Laws and the Workhouse

The idea of the workhouse had been around since at least the 14th century, but in the 17th century it became more popular. The poor were a financial burden on the parish and by denying 'out-relief' to the able-bodied and forcing them to work in order to survive, they could save money. In 1723 the Workhouse Test Act gave parishes the option to make the workhouse the only choice for those who were capable of work.

By the 1770s there were around two thousand such workhouses in the country, housing nearly one hundred thousand people. Inmates were set menial tasks such as spinning or sewing and had to adhere to strict rules. A few workhouses were run well. They were clean and offered basic education and health care. Other workhouses, however, were overcrowded and full of disease. In the 1750s social investigator Jonas Hanway discovered that the death rate amongst workhouse children in London was over ninety per cent. This meant some of the poor were prepared to starve rather than enter their walls.

The Relief of the Poor Act of 1782 enabled parishes to form unions known as Gilbert Unions to build and maintain larger workhouses to accommodate the infirmed and elderly. They were to find able-bodied workers employment with landowners, farmers and other employers who received allowances from the poor rates, and to give the labourers relief until work was found. However, not many of these unions were formed and by the 1830s most parishes had at least one workhouse.

THE POOR LAWS AND THE WORKHOUSE

The Poor Law Amendment Act of 1834 aimed to end all out-relief for the able-bodied. Poor Law Unions were formed from the fifteen thousand or so parishes in England and Wales and each Union had its central workhouse. This led to a further five hundred workhouses being built over the following few years. Ireland and Scotland were to set up similar schemes in the following decade.

Despite this Act many parishes still preferred to offer out-relief to those with sickness in the family, as it was more cost effective than boarding them in the workhouses. The 1844 Outdoor Relief Prohibitory Order reinforced the idea that all out-relief to the able-bodied poor be abolished.

George Cruikshank's original drawing of the young Oliver Twist asking for more

However, in 1846, of one million, three hundred and thirty thousand paupers, only one hundred and ninety-nine thousand were maintained in workhouses, of whom eighty-two thousand were considered to be able-bodied, leaving an estimated three hundred and seventy-five thousand of the able-bodied on outdoor relief.

The workhouse was not intended to be a pleasant place. Men, women, children, the sick, and the able-bodied were kept separate and were fed basic rations of gruel, bread and cheese. They were forced to wear rough uniforms and were only allowed to bathe under supervision once a week. Many of the able-bodied were given arduous or monotonous work such as stone-breaking or removing the hemp from telegraph wires. Another favourite was picking apart old rope known as oakum. Parents were allowed very little contact with their children, perhaps an hour or so a week on a Sunday.

In 1848, The Times suggested that ninety per cent of fourteen-year-old girls who left the workhouse ended up working as prostitutes. Although the law surrounding the age of consent was rather complicated at that time, in England the age was just ten! This was raised to twelve in 1861 and to thirteen in 1875, but it was not until 1885 that the Criminal Law Amendment raised the age of consent to sixteen.

Gradually, through various Acts and through the outrage of the more caring members of society, things began to improve in the workhouses.

THE POOR LAWS AND THE WORKHOUSE

The basic rations began to include more wholesome food and occasional treats and outings were allowed.

The Diseases Prevention Act of 1883 allowed for treatment of all in the workhouse infirmaries, not just the poor, and some began to operate as private hospitals. By the end of the century about thirty per cent of all those aged over seventy were in workhouses. This led in part to the introduction of the old age pension. See https://en.wikipedia.org/wiki/Workhouse

From 1913 onwards, the term 'workhouse' was replaced by 'Poor Law Institution', and in 1929 this changed again to 'Public Assistance Institution'.

Officially, the workhouse was abolished on the 1st of April 1930, but the buildings continued to be used to house the elderly, chronically sick, unmarried mothers and the homeless. Even after the National Health Service was formed in 1948, the former workhouse buildings continued to be utilised for the care of the old and those in need of constant medical care.

Gradually, some of the old workhouse buildings were demolished or began falling into decay, but many still exist as part of new hospitals, care homes, residential homes or business premises.

If you are interested in finding out more about the Poor Laws and workhouses, then www.workhouses.org.uk is an extremely informative website which includes detailed information about the various workhouses throughout the country.

Obtaining Poor Law and Workhouse Records

You may find that your ancestor spent time in the workhouse from one of the censuses or a birth certificate, but bearing in mind these are only a snapshot into their lives, it is possible that they did have a stint in the workhouse in between these years.

Find my Past has a selection of valuable records from many counties including the London Poor Law Records from 1581 to 1899. Ancestry also holds county records as well as London, England, Workhouse Admission and Discharge Records from 1659 to 1930, London, England, Poor Law and Board of Guardian Records from 1430 to 1930 and London, England, Selected Poor Law Removal and Settlement Records from 1828 to 1930.

In this instance, however, the best source of information is likely to be the local county archives. They will hold workhouse records as well as settlement certificates and other records that may indicate that your ancestor was affected by the Poor Laws. The National Archives website, discovery.nationalarchives.gov.uk will be useful here and the workhouses.org.uk website gives a list of all the archives of interest.

When most of us start to delve into our family history we are often hoping to find somebody rich or famous. The sad, but often more interesting truth is, we are far more likely to be descended from someone who experienced poverty, hunger and severe hardship during their lifetime!

CHAPTER 9

Death and Disease

In Britain in the 21st century if a member of our family dies, particularly if that person is not considered old, it is felt as a time of great loss and waste of a life. It is easy to think that it would have been easier for our ancestors because they experienced far more loss of life at an early age than we do now. However, as humans we are programmed to care for and look after our loved ones and this is a trait that has evolved in primates for millions of years. It makes no sense to believe that the loss we feel was not equal to the loss felt by our ancestors, however common the situation was.

The Middle Ages

Almost nothing was known about the causes of disease at this time. Most doctors believed as the Greeks had done, that illness was caused when the 'Four Humours' i.e., phlegm, black bile, yellow bile and blood became unbalanced. Demons, witches, the stars and bad smells were just a few of the reasons that the medieval population believed to be responsible.

There was some form of progress during this time though. Doctors developed the first painkillers in the form of opium, and wine was used as an antiseptic. It is now believed that medieval towns would have been cleaner than those of later times. Towns were less crowded and some even had public bath houses. Parliament passed the first law requiring people to keep the streets and rivers clean in 1388. However, none of these precautions could stop the spread of the most infectious and deadly diseases.

The Black Death or Plague swept across Europe between 1346 and 1353. It reached the shores of the British Isles in June 1348 via Dorset. Two months later it devastated Bristol, England's second largest city and major port. It hit London in September and spread its way across England into Wales, Ireland and eventually Scotland in 1350.

The Black Death was an epidemic of bubonic plague, a disease caused by the bacterium yersinia, spread by fleas. It is found in wild rats, usually black rats. It can take up to two weeks for the disease to destroy the entire population of the rat colony and for another three days the fleas lie dormant until the threat of starvation forces them to feed on humans. The bites cause buboes, swellings in the lymph nodes, hence the name bubonic plague.

In the cities, victims were thrown into large mass graves, as many as two hundred a day were 'disposed' of in this way.

With the rise of urban populations and the expansion of trade with Europe during the Middle Ages, the disease was able to spread quickly. Most people believed it to be the will of God who was punishing them for their sins.

In 1349 the King ordered that the polluted and overcrowded city of London be cleaned up, but all the street cleaners had died of the disease!

The Black Death was not prejudiced in its victims. It affected both rich and poor, killing Archbishops as well as peasants. It is thought to have killed between a third and a half of the population, some rural villages losing as much as eighty to ninety per cent of their inhabitants.

By 1350 the Black Death had run its course in Britain, but it returned sporadically (although less destructively) until the late 17th century. Later outbreaks were particularly fatal for children and young people. It's sad to think of all the parents who must have wept for the loss of their little ones.

During the Middle Ages if you survived the Black Death, it was no guarantee that you would survive into old age. There were many other dangers that could prove fatal.

In the early 14th century, there was 'The Great Famine'. From 1300 Europe experienced a 'Little Ice Age' and between 1315 and 1322 there was incredibly heavy and prolonged rainfall. Farmers struggled to produce crops and between ten and fifteen per cent of the English population died of starvation.

It is estimated that between twenty and thirty per cent of children (and quite possibly a lot more) died under the age of seven during the mediaeval period. Diseases such as measles, whooping cough, smallpox and tuberculosis were just a few of the many that were the cause of such a great loss of young life. Malnutrition and infections were common and a mother who was undernourished would not have provided sufficient immunity in her breast milk to sustain her infant.

Even in wealthy families it is estimated from records that between 1330 and 1479 one third of all children of Dukes died before the age of five.

Childbirth itself was fraught with danger. Breech births, hemorrhaging and simple exhaustion could prove fatal and post-natal infection was common.

Life itself was hazardous during these times. Simply travelling from one place to another could cause death from exposure or violence, and there were many accidents caused by hunting or lack of safety in the home.

Hospitals have been around since the Middle Ages. In 1247 the Priory of St Mary of Bethlehem was founded in Bishopsgate by Simon Fitzmary, the Sheriff of London. It was originally developed as a place of healing for sick paupers, but by the turn of the 15th century it was largely dedicated to the treatment of the 'insane'. This not only included those with mental health problems, but also those with learning difficulties, dementia and epilepsy. The regime consisted of punishment and religious worship, both of which

'Bedlam' from William Hogarth's 'A Rake's Progress' c. 1733

were considered to be useful tools in aiding recovery. This institution came to be known as Bedlam.

However, the vast majority of those both mentally and physically ill would not have been institutionalised. Their treatment would have included an array of 'cures'. Some like the application of leeches is now realised to have some benefit, whilst others such as whipping to earn God's forgiveness were clearly steeped in superstition and of no benefit to the patient.

The 16th to 18th Centuries

During this era people were still unaware about germs and how diseases were spread. Filthy water and faeces would be thrown into the streets and personal hygiene such as hand washing was not deemed to be necessary.

The Plague was still affecting England during the 16th century. Of those affected at this time about half died. Over a quarter of London's population was wiped out.

Between 1643 and 1652 the Civil War raged across England. The conflict left some thirty-four thousand Parliamentarians and fifty thousand Royalists dead, while at least one hundred thousand men and women died from war-related diseases, bringing the total death toll in England to almost two hundred thousand, about four per cent of the population at that time. More died in Scotland, and far more in Ireland.

In 1665 another great outbreak of Plague occurred. It began in London in the poor, overcrowded parish of St. Giles-in-the-Field. By June more than six thousand people had died and just two months later the toll had risen to more than thirty thousand. This was fifteen per cent of London's population at the time. By the end of the year the disease was almost eradicated, and the Great Fire of London the following year, which destroyed much of the filth ridden city, was a blessing in disguise as London was cleansed.

Before antibiotics, bacterial diseases such as syphilis and cholera could often prove fatal. Cholera was caused by

DEATH AND DISEASE

drinking contaminated water. Before the installation of proper sewerage systems, outbreaks were commonplace.

Another huge killer was typhus. In the filthy crowded conditions of the cities and the lack of hygiene of the majority, body lice were common. If a person scratched and the faeces of the lice entered the bloodstream, then it was often a swift and painful death. Many criminals, some in jail for petty crimes, died in the squalid conditions of the city prisons.

Smallpox was also common. Queen Elizabeth herself contracted it in 1562 when she was twenty-nine years old. Although she survived, it left her bald, and she had to cover the scars on her face with thick white make up (made from white lead and egg whites!) for the rest of her life.

Dysentery, scarlet fever, influenza, pneumonia and all the other aforementioned diseases were still common causes of death in children.

'The King's Evil' was the name given to scrofula, the swelling of the bones and lymphatic glands in the neck caused by tuberculosis. In England and France from the time of Edward the Confessor it was believed that the disease could be cured by a royal touch.

Subsequently, monarchs would hold ceremonies where hundreds of people suffering from the disease would kneel before them and touch their hand.

James I thought it mere superstition, but after the return of the monarchy following the Commonwealth period, Charles II restarted the ceremony. The ceremony concluded with a reading from the bible, prayers and a blessing. Then the King's hands were washed.

In 1712 Queen Anne touched Samuel Johnson who was then a two-year old boy. The practice ended with Anne, the final Stuart monarch, but continued in France until 1825.

Perhaps more surprising than the aforementioned diseases, malaria was the cause of many deaths around the Thames during this period. The swampy theatre district of Southwark was particularly at risk.

Accidents were still common. Drowning in wells and bathtubs was the most reported accidental death in children under the age of five.

The Industrial Revolution

Towards the end of the 18th century the Industrial Revolution was beginning to take hold in Britain. Villages and small cottage industries were being rapidly replaced by towns, cities and factories. It was a time when there was little or no regard for the workers' health or safety, and danger was everywhere.

Workers had to endure long hours of labour, machinery was often exposed, and conditions were hot and crowded. Exhaustion could lead to a lack of concentration, which in turn led to a higher risk of injury.

Children were employed to clean up, moving between the machines. The long hours meant that during the winter months, workers would see no daylight. As well as the many accidents amongst the children, rickets due to lack of vitamin D obtained mainly from sunlight, were common.

Until 1842 children as young as five could be 'bought' to work down the mines. Because of the cramped conditions they could develop distorted bodies and lung disease as well as risking death from the causes mentioned below.

Likewise, until as late as 1875, young children could be used as chimney sweeps. This could not only cause the obvious problems of such an occupation, but also a disease that my own great-great grandfather and his father before him had died of at a relatively early age – chimney sweep's cancer.

This was a form of cancer that affected the scrotum, and was caused by the friction of filthy, sweaty clothes when sweeps were sifting soot. The cancer began as a superficial sore with hard, rising edges that worsened over time. The only known cure was the removal of the infected organ. Few sweeps (including my ancestors), with their general mistrust of all forms of institution, were willing to put themselves through such an ordeal.

Meanwhile the ever-increasing number of factories required more and more power, and the coal mining industry expanded to accommodate this. The dangers for overworked, underpaid miners were just as hazardous as those working in factories. Many were killed by gas, explosions, or due to tunnels caving in.

During the 19th century well-meaning reformers brought about change. Various Factory Acts between 1819 and 1847 limited the hours worked by children and women. By 1874 no factory workers were allowed to work more than fifty-six and a half hours per week.

"A Dreadful Shock to the Nerves" by John Leech first published in Punch in 1846

Despite the horrors of industrial labour, millions flooded into the towns and cities seeking work. This kept wages low and exploitation by the middle-class factory owners was the norm. The influx of so many people caused even more overcrowding and poor sanitation.

Industrial Britain was hit by several outbreaks of cholera in the years 1831–32, 1848–49, 1854 and 1867. In the early 19th century, the Thames was an open sewer system and was also used as a source of drinking water. It was not until Dr. John Snow proved that disease was spread by bacteria rather than smell, and 'the Great Stink' in the summer of

1858, that plans for a proper sewerage system that diverted waste to the Thames estuary were drawn up by Joseph Bazalgette. The sewers were completed around 1870 and are still in use today.

Smallpox was still around despite Edward Jenner's vaccine of 1798. Many people were either unaware or wary of it.

Typhoid, another water born disease and typhus were still very prominent, particularly in the cities.

Tuberculosis is a highly contagious disease caused by inhaling droplets of sputum from an infected person. It was the highest cause of death in the cities, and it is estimated that it was responsible for a third of all deaths between 1800 and 1850.

However, by the end of the 19th century, with the discovery of the need for better sanitation and hygiene and with the rise of the trade unions, the causes and number of deaths were on the decline.

20th Century

During the late 19th and early 20th centuries more vaccines were discovered for diseases such as diphtheria, tetanus, whooping cough and tuberculosis, followed in the 1950s by the Polio vaccine. By 1980 it was announced that smallpox, such a common and virulent disease in the past, had been eradicated worldwide.

Better working conditions meant a safer working environment and an increase in wages meant better nutrition for the working classes.

By far the biggest concentrated loss of life during the 20th century was caused by war.

The figures relating to British casualties of the First World War are very hazy. Estimates vary according to different sources. Between seven hundred thousand and one million soldiers lost their lives whilst an estimated two million were wounded. Civilian losses are estimated to be about thirty-one thousand.

But as the war ended and peace was on the horizon, the worst global pandemic in history to that date struck – the Spanish Flu. It is estimated to have killed over a quarter of a million Britain's alone, and between fifty and one hundred million worldwide, but by mid-1919 the disease disappeared as quickly and unexpectedly as it had arrived.

Estimates of deaths in the Second World War also differ. Somewhere between three hundred thousand and four hundred thousand military personnel died and between sixty thousand and seventy thousand civilians.

The contrast between the two wars is noticeable. Roughly half as many soldiers died, but twice as many civilians. This is a devastating number, but only represents about one per cent of the British population, fewer than the estimated two percent who died in the first World War and even fewer than

DEATH AND DISEASE

those who lost their lives three hundred years earlier during the English Civil War.

During the 20th century and up to today the causes of death and disease have for the most part, dramatically changed.

Infant mortality rates at the beginning of the century were nearly thirty times higher than they are now.

With the continuing worldwide research into health, people are living much longer. In 1901 only twenty per cent of the population lived beyond the age of sixty-five, today it is around eighty per cent. This has meant a shift in the causes of death.

Due to the discovery of antibiotics and further vaccination programs, many infectious diseases have been all but eradicated. Our better understanding of hygiene means the likes of cholera, typhus and typhoid are diseases of the past.

Today the leading causes of death are heart failure, dementia and cancer.

Of course, recently the world has experienced the COVID 19 pandemic. At the time of writing, the World Health Organisation estimates that it has killed almost six and a half million people worldwide, and there have been over six hundred million confirmed cases. This, of course, is probably not the whole story, as many cases go unreported, or even unnoticed in asymptomatic cases. The figures for the UK are an estimated twenty-three and a half million cases with one hundred and eighty-eighty thousand deaths.

The majority of these fatalities occurred before the vaccination programs were rolled out, and one can only speculate how much more devastating the virus would have been, had we not had the technology to develop these vaccines. Also, COVID, unlike the Spanish flu, mainly affects older people, so is much less likely to cause a decline in new births.

However, the pandemic currently shows no sign of dying out as swiftly as the Spanish flu. The herd immunity at that time meant the spread of the virus was uninterrupted by medical intervention, and therefore, having affected as many as was possible, it was eradicated swiftly.

So, it seems that no matter how far we think we have come in the war against disease, it may never be far enough.

Obtaining Information About the Diseases and Deaths of Your Ancestors

It is easy to discover what your ancestors died of if they passed away after the introduction of death certificates. However, sometimes the cause may be something unfamiliar to us. There are several websites that give lists of old names for modern diseases, but it is probably best to just Google it. Some of these illnesses are a product of their time.

Finding instances of disease and death prior to the introduction of registration is really potluck.

Most parish records just give burial dates with no mention of a cause of death. Occasionally, particularly in cases of infectious diseases such as smallpox, the cause may be recorded. I have found this written in the margins on several occasions.

Sometimes there might be obvious clues. If a mother dies shortly after the birth of a child, it might be safe to assume there were complications or an infection involved. Of course, there is no certainty. If several members of a family die close together at the time of an epidemic, again this could be an indicator.

Most illnesses and accidents that do not result in loss of life are rarely going to be recorded, but occasionally you might get lucky.

Two examples are shown below:

A record of a child who had been 'touched' by the King – Mary survived, perhaps the King did have a 'magic' touch!

As George Ruddell, aged 9 years, living in East-street, was crossing the Old Kent-road on Saturday, he was knocked down and run over by a horse and cart, and sustained a fracture of the thigh.

Taken from the London Press, December 21st 1867

The best sources of newspaper records, if you have a subscription, are Find My Past or newspapers.com, which is linked to Ancestry. A 7-day trial is available with a subscription of £49.99 every six months after that. Another useful source is www.britishnewspaperarchive.co.uk. These records are available by paid subscription or pay as you go credits. If you can get to local libraries or archives, you have an even better chance of finding a juicy titbit about an ancestor. However, these records are often not indexed or digitised, so unless you are aware of the date of a particular event, it can be very laborious, working your way through pages of microfilm. There are other websites that concentrate on particular newspapers and areas, and a good source of information on these can be found at www.nationalarchives.gov.uk which has a newspaper research guide.

You might be lucky enough to find the last resting place of an ancestor. Of course, you can wander around churchyards if you know the parish in which they were buried.

Also, as mentioned before, websites that might be of use are:

www.deceasedonline.com
www.findagrave.com
www.billiongraves.com

However, bearing in mind that most people were buried without headstones and that the stones break and disappear over time, it is unusual to find very old graves.

DEATH AND DISEASE

There is one last thing to mention about burial records and headstones. Don't take the age given too literally and end up basing other research on it. These ages are not set in stone (not metaphorically anyway – if you pardon the pun).

As with the censuses, particularly in older people, ages might have been forgotten, or those left behind simply may not know. In a time before old age pension, the only age that really mattered was twenty-one, when you became an adult and were able to leave an apprenticeship or get married without parental consent. After that, age became pretty much irrelevant. It was just a number!

CHAPTER 10

Education and Apprenticeships

The History of Education in Britain

Formal education was first seen in Britain at the time of the Roman Occupation, but as with most of the advancements that the Romans brought, this almost certainly disappeared when they left.

The first known school was established in Canterbury in the year 598 by St. Augustine who needed an establishment to teach priests Latin.

'Grammar schools' as they were then known, gradually expanded their curricula to include mathematics and science.

During the Viking invasions which began at the end of the 8th century, education once more fell into decline, but after the Norman conquest of 1066, it flourished and began to become more secular. By the end of the 13th century Universities began to develop.

EDUCATION AND APPRENTICESHIPS

During this time more 'independent schools' became established. The word independent meant independent from the church, not from the state as it has come to mean today. These brought education to the children of the 'upper classes', but also began to include charitable organisations for the poor.

Although it is not possible to be completely accurate, it is estimated that in the 16th century only twenty per cent of adult males could sign their name and only five per cent of women.

Of course, this varied enormously between the classes. Aristocrats, gentry and rich merchants were almost totally literate by 1600, but most labourers could not read at all.

In Elizabethan times the Renaissance brought new ideas about philosophy and art, and some schools began to incorporate these into their teachings.

By the end of the 17th century, it is estimated that the amount of those who could sign their name had risen to fifty per cent of men and twenty-five per cent of women.

By the beginning of the 18th century the curriculum in schools was beginning to take on its modern form and included mathematics, geography, modern languages and science.

However, schooling was far from within the reach of everyone. There were parish schools funded by charities and wealthy

"February – Cutting Weather – Squally" by George Cruikshank 1839

patrons, but they were not in every village and with the growth of urbanisation most children from poorer families received no education at all. If a child went to school, he could not earn any money for the family, and his income could often mean the difference between eating and starvation.

Girls in particular were unlikely to receive any schooling. If they did have some form of education, it was taught by governesses and would often have included less academia and more practical work such as sewing or spinning.

In the 1780s the Sunday School movement began. This allowed boys who worked all week to at least have some form of education. These schools were initially designed for the poorer 'workhouse' children to teach them not only to read and write, but to instill Christianity into them.

EDUCATION AND APPRENTICESHIPS

In the 1830s, Parliament began to get involved and money was put aside to build free schools for poorer children.

At the beginning of the Victorian age, it was estimated that more than one in three Englishmen were illiterate and half of all women. Even in wealthier families, girls were mostly taught at home.

In the 1840s the 'Ragged Schools' were becoming popular. These were charitable schools for destitute children and catered mainly for the urban poor of the industrial cities. The Ragged School Union was established and some resources for free clothing and even lodging were provided. By 1870, at their peak, there were two hundred and fifty of these schools in London and one hundred outside the capital.

In 1857 the Industrial Schools Act was intended to solve problems of juvenile delinquency, by lawfully removing poor

The RAGGED SCHOOL.
In West Street (late Chick Lane) Smithfield.
Drawn by George Cruikshank about 1843-4.

and neglected children from their home environment to a boarding school.

In 1870 a new Act was passed that began to make provision for all children to have elementary education. In 1880 it was made compulsory for all children aged between the ages of five and ten to attend school. Because poor families still needed the income from their children more than they needed them to be educated, employed children who were under the age of thirteen were obliged to have a certificate indicating that they had reached a certain level of education. This was not always adhered to.

In 1893 the school-leaving age was raised to eleven and then to twelve in 1899.

Various Parliamentary Acts followed which culminated in the system we have today. Now less than one per cent of all adults in Britain are totally illiterate, although there are many who still struggle with reading despite the level of education now attainable.

Education for the disabled

Prior to the 1870s for the blind, the deaf and others with disabilities education was rare. A few charities had set up institutions particularly for the blind and deaf, but generally they were excluded from the system.

In 1874, the London School Board established a class for the deaf at a public elementary school and in 1875 it did the same for blind children. By 1888 there were fourteen centres for the deaf and twenty-three centres for the blind attached to ordinary schools, catering for about five hundred children. The following year, the London Board made the first arrangements for teaching blind children in its elementary schools. A few other boards made provision for the deaf and blind, but it was the exception rather than the norm.

In 1893, the Elementary Education (Blind and Deaf Children) Act required school authorities (boards, district councils or school attendance committees) to make provision for the education of blind and deaf children resident in their area, who were not receiving suitable elementary education.

However, unlike the blind and deaf, other physically disabled and the mentally disabled children had no large organisations to fight their cause. After the 1870 Education Act these children were often incorporated into the normal elementary school system which caused problems.

The Royal Commission on the Blind and Deaf, which also covered other special needs, made a report in 1889 that made a distinction between three different levels of mental disability – the feeble-minded, imbeciles and idiots. It stated that the feeble-minded should receive special education separately from ordinary children, that imbeciles should attend institutions where they could, and receive an education concentrating on sensory and physical development and the improvement of speech, and that idiots should be considered to be uneducable.

By 1896 there were twenty-four special schools in London attended by nine hundred pupils, and by the end of the century schools for 'defective' children had been established by six other boards.

Apprenticeships

Apprenticeships in England date back to medieval times when the craft guilds were established. Guilds were originally set up from the 10th century onwards when merchants formed alliances to band together for protection on their trading routes. From these merchant guilds the craft guilds developed, allowing tradesmen to set rules and restrictions within their own trade to protect standards and quality of craftsmanship. These guilds often relied on the apprenticeship system and people from the higher classes would sometimes send their children away to live with host families to learn a trade.

At first there were no strict rules or guidelines, but in 1563 the Statute of Artificers and Apprentices was passed. This regulated the system and forbade anyone to practice a trade without first having served a minimum of seven years as an apprentice.

The Poor Relief Act of 1601 allowed authorities to bind a child to a master and apprenticeships began to be a way of instruction for more than just the wealthier classes. This was mostly to stop the child being a drain on the resources of the parish, which was often the case with illegitimate and orphaned children. At first children as young as seven could be apprenticed. Most apprentices were boys, but some girls were accepted in trades such as seamstresses, bakers and stationers.

At first the master was obliged to give the apprentice board, lodging and clothing, but little else. The child was originally bound until the age of twenty-four, this being reduced to twenty-one in 1778. During this time the 'boys' were forbidden to marry. However, 'girls' could be released from their apprenticeships early if they married. After all, a married woman was the responsibility of her husband and society was freed from any accountability for her financial and moral well-being!

In 1747, William Hogarth made a series of engravings called "Industry and Idleness" which consisted of twelve plates depicting an industrious apprentice and an idle apprentice.

On the following pages are four of them. Each image included a verse from Proverbs in the Bible, which gives us an idea of how the work ethic and the importance of God played a big part in Georgian Britain.

In 1801, a Parliamentary Act required that apprenticeship registers should be kept, and in 1802, Peel's Factory Act was passed. It mainly dealt with the ill treatment of children in the ever-increasing factory system, but it also considered the welfare of apprentices. Employers had to provide instruction in reading, writing and arithmetic during at least the first four years of the seven years of apprenticeship and the hours that the apprentices could work were limited.

"The Idle 'Prentice at Play in the Church Yard during Divine Service"

"The Industrious 'Prentice performing the duty of a Christian"

EDUCATION AND APPRENTICESHIPS

"The Idle 'Prentice Executed at Tyburn"

"The Industrious 'Prentice Lord-Mayor of London"

In 1814, the 1563 Statute was repealed and removed the seven years minimum requirement.

Legislation continued to improve conditions, but even from the earliest and harshest forms of apprenticeship, it was still often a way that an otherwise poor and unskilled child could learn a trade that would put him or her very slightly above the very lowest members of society.

Unfortunately, the practice by the parish of forcing children into apprenticeships to learn a trade was sometimes lax, and the children were sent to farms, private homes or shops merely to become unpaid servants.

However, many were lucky enough to learn a trade and most of those spent time as a journeyman at the end of their term of apprenticeship. This meant they were still hired by the master craftsmen but were paid a wage. Sometimes the journeymen went on to become master tradesmen themselves, but unfortunately others never acquired their own workshop.

Compulsory apprenticeship was finally abolished in 1844, which coincided with the introduction of the Ragged schools, but even today it is a useful way to learn a trade or occupation.

Obtaining Information About Education and Apprenticeships

If you're trying to find where your ancestor was educated, Ancestry has a varied collection of school and university

EDUCATION AND APPRENTICESHIPS

registers, in particular the London, England, School Admissions and Discharges, 1840–1911 which includes over one million pupils from eight hundred and forty-three schools.

The 'National School Registers 1870–1914' on Find my Past, an example of which is shown above, covers (at the time of writing) over seven million records from forty-one counties in England and Wales. Find my Past also has records of teachers from 1914 to 1948.

For records of Ragged Schools and other charitable organisations, it is more likely that you will find records (if they still exist) in the local archives or a trip to the National Archives might be useful.

For residential schools your first clue will often be in the censuses. If you have the name of the institution, then in my experience it is highly likely that you will find something online or in the local library about it.

Recently my research took me to a boy who was, in 1871, a pupil at the Boy's Farm Home in East Barnet. By checking online, I was able to establish that this was a part of the

London Boys' Home, initially founded in 1858 in Euston Road, London for destitute and wayward boys to teach them a trade. The Boy's Farm Home, as its name suggests, focused on farm work. Unfortunately, none of the admission records still exist, so it was not possible to find under what circumstances he was admitted. However, he was a domestic gardener all his life and died in 1923 in a very pretty village in Sussex leaving an estate of £122 7s 11d (which is over £5000 in today's money).

Registers were kept from very early on regarding the duties masters had to pay for apprentices that were not bound to them by the parish. The UK Register of Duties Paid for Apprentices' Indentures, 1710–1811 on Ancestry is an extremely useful tool (an example of which is below). However, if your ancestor was bound to a master by the parish, then it is more likely that, if the records still survive, they will be found in local archives. From 1836 they are also available at the National Archives in the 'Poor Law union indexes and papers'.

EDUCATION AND APPRENTICESHIPS

Ancestry also has Merchant Navy apprenticeship records, 'Articles of Clerkship' relating to contracts between an apprentice clerk and an attorney and extracted apprenticeship records from West Yorkshire.

Find my Past has the registers of duties paid by masters under 'Britain, Country Apprentices 1710–1808' as well as several other useful catalogues containing apprenticeships including extracts from London, Dorset, Gloucester, York and Somerset, and various London guild registers.

If your ancestor may have been apprenticed at one of London's livery companies, then a very useful site is www.londonroll.org.

Sometimes there would be disputes between apprentices and their masters and sometimes parents would simply refuse to let their children go. Records of these disagreements may be found in Parish Overseer's records in local archives if they have survived and you are lucky enough to find them.

Sometimes you find something out by chance. Recently I found a mention of an apprenticeship in a Last Will and Testament. Whilst I couldn't find a copy of the apprenticeship record itself, it did confirm by the trade that my research was going in the right direction.

As with most of your research, finding where your ancestor was (or *if* he or she was) educated or apprenticed, is partly hard work and partly luck.

CHAPTER 11

Geographical Mobility and Population Growth

General Overview

The further you go back with your research, the more likely it is that you will find that your ancestors stayed in the same place for generations. As previously pointed out, most people were poor, and the Poor Laws would not allow the movement of people between towns and villages without documentation, so it was easier for most people to stay in the town or village where they were born.

Some people would have had trades, such as blacksmiths and bakers, and these trades would have been passed down from father to son. It is likely that they would have provided for the same town or village through generations. Most, however, would have been casual labourers working on local farms and

"Over London" by Gustav Dore

earning what they could when it was available. Agricultural work was seasonal and often poorly paid.

With the dawn of the Industrial Revolution, things began to change. New machinery on farms could do the work of a dozen men and many moved from the rural areas into the ever-expanding towns and cities, their already precarious choice of living made even harder. Factory jobs employed men, women and children all year round, so despite the often squalid and cramped conditions of urban life, it was considered preferable to starvation. Consequently, the population movement within England became far more common.

Other factors that lured people to the towns and cities were the better chance of education for their children in Sunday Schools and the belief that the houses were better built.

As well as people moving within England, there also began to be more migration. This was sometimes due to the transportation of criminals, sometimes through necessity and sometimes through choice. There was a whole new world waiting for them across the oceans and many took a chance and ventured forth.

From the early 19th century, the Irish had been coming to England and the USA, and the potato blight of the 1840s saw an estimated one million Irish leave their shores for a new life.

During the late 18th and into the middle of the 19th centuries the Scottish Land Clearances, which saw tenant farmers being forced from their homes, meant that the Scots too were forced to flee. Many emigrated to Australia, New Zealand or Canada, but some moved across the border to England.

Between 1700 and 1750, the population of England stayed relatively stable. Then, between 1750 and 1850, it more

"Emigrants Landing at the Queen's Wharf Melbourne" by Nicholas Chevalier

than doubled. This, however, was not just due to the arrival of the Scots and Irish. Indeed, during this time many English families were emigrating to the British Colonies themselves, which would, to a degree have counteracted it.

In fact, the combined population of England, Scotland, Ireland and Wales in 1801 was an estimated eighteen million; by 1851 it was twenty-seven million. The death rate was decreasing as children were more likely to survive infancy. There was as a better awareness of the need for sanitation, along with the introduction of some inoculations.

Another factor was that people were beginning to marry younger. With a steadier income it was easier for people to set up home together and earlier marriages meant more children. So, there were simply more people being born than were dying.

In 1700 an estimated seventeen per cent of the English population lived in urban areas, by 1801 this had increased to around twenty-eight per cent, and by 1851 over half lived in the towns and cities.

Of course, one thing that made movement from one place to another much easier was the great advancements in transportation. With the building of the railways, a journey that would have taken days could be done in hours.

Prior to the increase in geographical mobility following the Industrial Revolution, other factors played a part. For centuries religious belief had led to discrimination against

The Great Western Railway Terminus, at Paddington, London – Designed by I K Brunel and M D Wyatt from The Illustrated London News, 8 July 1854

both Protestants and Catholics depending on the monarch at any given time, and in the early 18th century more than fifty thousand French Protestants or Huguenots fled to our shores to escape their own persecution.

Whilst on the subject of religion, it is worth mentioning here that parish records for English Catholics are not the easiest to find online. Ancestry and Find My Past have a few, as does www.thegenealogist.co.uk but it is more likely that local research will be of further use on this subject, although the websites www.catholicfhs.wordpress.com may also be of some help.

If you are looking for Jewish ancestors, then www.jewishgen.org is particularly useful.

To sum up, there has always been some mobility within, as well as to and from England, but prior to 1800, you are much more likely to have ancestors that stayed put.

If you can trace a surname back to the 1851 census where it first gives a place of birth, then there is a reasonable chance that you may have found the village or at least an adjoining village or town where your ancestors had lived for generations. Of course, as with any other research, take care. Forenames were not very varied, and your line might have married and moved away, with a cousin with the same name still residing in the one you are looking at.

As mentioned before, villages and towns are not always within the same county or boundary over time. Make allowances for this. A useful source for checking historical counties is 'Great Britain, Atlas and Index of Parish Registers' on Ancestry.

One last website worth mentioning if you want to know more about the places and times that your ancestors lived is www.british-history.ac.uk. This site has a wealth of information from primary and secondary sources relating to British history from 1300 onwards including maps and gazetteers, and it can help to give you a real insight into the lives of those who came before.

CHAPTER 12

Scotland and Ireland

Scotland

Tracing your Scottish ancestors is easier than it once was, as Ancestry and Find My Past now hold extensive records. If you can't find what you're looking for there, then the website www.scotlandspeople.gov.uk can be useful. However, this site does not offer subscriptions, and although access to some of the indexes is free of charge, to actually look further and find out if the name you are looking at is the right one, you need to buy credits. Viewing each image can cost over £1 and there is no guarantee that you have found the right one, meaning a lot of money wasted.

Of course, if you live close enough to visit the National Records of Scotland facilities in Edinburgh, then you will have access to all the records without having to pay, except for a small charge for copying documents. As with all records offices it is advisable to visit their website first and register

"Edinburgh Castle and the Grassmarket from Candlemaker Row" by Henry G. Duguid

as a user. The website, www.nrscotland.gov.uk, also gives lots of information on what is available and how to find it.

The first time I undertook Scottish research was for a client with ancestors in the Highlands and as I live on the south coast of England, visiting the archives would have proved very costly. However, after finding that I was spending a lot of my client's money on the Scotland's People website, I subscribed to the Highland Family History Society at: https://highlandfhs.org

I emailed them regarding my particular needs, and the treasurer John Durham kindly telephoned me and gave me some very useful advice. He put me in touch with a society member, who visits the Edinburgh Archives regularly and carries out research for clients at a very reasonable rate.

She was a godsend enabling me to save my clients' money and removing the frustration of paying for several wrong document images, before (if lucky) finding the correct one. This is often the case because there are far less surnames in Scotland than in England and Wales, so if you are searching for a Donald Mackenzie and know little else about them, the chances of you stumbling across the right one straight away are quite small.

I am very keen on using family history societies and they are well worth checking out. As I have mentioned before they can be a very useful tool to varying degrees and they all offer different services, but in my experience the good ones have provided a wealth of help and information. The Scottish Association of Family History Societies at www.safhs.org.uk provides a comprehensive list.

If you are content with transcripts, rather than images of original documents (bearing in mind the possible inaccuracies through human error), then there are Scottish birth, marriage and death records and census records on Ancestry and familysearch.org. Find My Past also has transcripts of the censuses and a limited amount of birth, marriage and death records, including Roman Catholic records. Ancestry holds some other original documentation, so if you check through all the displayed records for your ancestor, you may come across something unexpected such as their time working on a trade ship, or their school admission dates.

Like England and Wales, the censuses began in 1841 and gives the same information. Some later censuses give extras like how many windows a dwelling had and whether the individual spoke Gaelic or Gaelic and English, all snippets that give a more rounded picture of your ancestor. The transcripts are available up until 1901 on Ancestry and Find My Past.

To find a 1911 census it is once again a matter of going to the Scotland's People website and buying credits or visiting the National or Local Archives. Again, you may be lucky and find someone who can do this for you.

The official registers of birth, marriage and death were not introduced in Scotland until 1855. The good news is that if you are able to find them then they give a much wider amount of information than those of England and Wales.

As well as all the information you can find on England and Wales certificates, the Scottish birth and death records give an actual time of the event and the mother's maiden name (preceded by M S). The birth records also give a date and place of the parent's marriage, and the death records give the marital status of the deceased. The marriage records give the names of the couple's mothers and their maiden names.

All of these 'extras' can help to confirm that you have the right person.

Overleaf are examples of post 1855 Scottish records:

The bad news is that prior to 1855, parish registers for the Church of Scotland were not kept nearly as fastidiously as those in England and Wales. It is possible to trace families

(Page 27.)

1861. BIRTHS in the District of Lochbroom in the County of Ross.

No.	Name and Surname	When and Where Born	Sex	Name, Surname, & Rank or Profession of Father. Name, and Maiden Surname of Mother. Date and Place of Marriage.	Signature and Qualification of Informant, and Residence, if out of the House in which the Birth occurred.	When and Where Registered, and Signature of Registrar.
79	Isabella Reid Mackenzie	1861 October Tenth 1h-5m Ullapool Lochbroom	F	Peter Mackenzie Merchant Mary Mackenzie M.S. Reid 1860, August 1st Garrabost, Lewis	Peter Mackenzie Father (Present)	1861 October 20th At Lochbroom Mundo McLay Registrar
80	Mary Munro	1861 October Thirty first 8h-5m Morefield Lochbroom	F	Duncan Munro Fisherman Christina Munro M.S. Urquhart 1848, November 30th Ullapool	Duncan Munro His Mark + Father (Present) Mundo McLay Witness	1861 November 6th At Lochbroom Mundo McLay Registrar
81	Kenneth Maclean	1861 November First 9h-5m Ullapool Lochbroom	M	Murdoch McLean Mason Janet Maclean M.S. Maclean 1861, January 3rd Ullapool	Murdoch McLean Father (Present)	1861 November 11th At Lochbroom Mundo McLay Registrar

Mundo McLay, Registrar.

(Page 27.)

1908. MARRIAGES in the District of Inverness in the County of Inverness.

No.	When, Where, and How Married	Signature of Parties. Rank or Profession, Whether Single or Widowed, and Relationship (if any).	Age	Usual Residence	Name, Surname, and Rank or Profession of Father. Name, and Maiden Surname of Mother.	If a regular Marriage, Signatures of officiating Minister and Witnesses. If irregular, Date of Conviction, Decree of Declaration, or Sheriff's Warrant.	When and Where Registered, and Signature of Registrar.
53 B.	1908 on the Twenty fourth day of April at 1 Huntly Street, Inverness. After Banns, according to the forms of the Church of Scotland	(Signed) Donald Young Sister-Daughter (Widower) (Signed) Annie McKenzie Domestic Servant (Spinster)	38 24	67 Muirtown Street, Inverness 67 Muirtown Street, Inverness	James Young Shoemaker (deceased) Mary Young M.S. Young (deceased) Hector Mackenzie Railway Surfaceman (deceased) Annie Mackenzie M.S. McAskill (deceased)	(Signed) G. John Leckerd Parish Minister (Signed) Henry Steel Witness Margaret Steel Witness	1908 April 27th at Inverness J. Macdonald asst. Registrar
54 B.	1908 on the Twenty eighth day of April at Roman Catholic Chapel Inverness. After Banns, according to the forms of the Roman Catholic Church	(Signed) Donald McDonald Cragsman (Bachelor) (Signed) Eliza Dunbar Domestic Servant (Spinster)	31 22	Tyler Street Forres 33 High Street Forres	Angus McDonald Shepherd (deceased) Catherine McDonald M.S. McKinnon Alexander Dunbar Labourer Ann Dunbar M.S. Shop	(Signed) Alexander Bisset Priest (Signed) John Ross Witness Helen Dunbar Witness	1908 April 29th at Inverness J. Macdonald asst. Registrar

J. MacBean Registrar.

SCOTLAND & IRELAND

back a long way, but it is really a matter of luck. Again, as Scottish names are less varied even if you find a record, there is usually only a sparse amount of information available, so no guarantee that you have the right one. A particularly valuable resource for finding where these records are available is the National Library of Scotland website at www.nls.uk.

Below is a pre-1855 death record.

If you are searching for Catholic ancestors, then as well as Find My Past, the Scottish Catholic Archives in Edinburgh (www.scottishcatholicarchives.org.uk) will give you an indication as to what is available and where.

Another very useful place to visit when tracing your Scottish ancestors is the Scottish Genealogy Society which is also based in Edinburgh.

Their website is www.scotsgenealogy.com and it has a lot of information on where records can be obtained.

One final online destination that I would like to mention here is http://edina.ac.uk/stat-acc-scot which has the statistical accounts for Scotland from 1791 to 1845. It has detailed descriptions of many Scottish towns which put real flesh on the bones of your ancestors. Sites like this and www.british-history.ac.uk provide information that is every bit as important in my work as finding names and dates. It brings a whole new aspect to family history research, and I thoroughly recommend it.

Ireland

Researching Irish ancestry can bring about its own problems. Between 1800 and 1922 Ireland was a part of the UK. During the civil war in 1922 the Public Record Office was burned down, and many historical documents were destroyed including census returns, Church of Ireland parish registers and wills and testamentary records. However, it is not all

"A Boating Party in Cork Harbour" by George Mounsey 1840

bad news. Some records did survive, and many records and transcripts were not housed in the Public Records Office.

There is actually still a wealth of information out there and many websites that can aid genealogical research. The following list covers those I recommend. Remember that this list is not exhaustive, and a little time spent googling occasionally brings up surprising information. To get you started though (and they may well be all you need), the following websites are extremely informative:

www.ancestry.co.uk (click on the Card Catalogue and then click on Ireland)

www.findmypast.com (click on the A-Z of Record Collections and then click on Ireland)

www.irish-genealogy-toolkit.com

www.nli.ie *The National Library of Ireland*

www.theirisharchives.com *The Irish Archives*

www.ancestryireland.com *Ulster Historical Foundation*

www.celticcousins.net

www.nifhs.org *The Northern Ireland Family History Group*

www.familyhistory.ie *The Genealogical Society of Ireland (Irish Republic)*

www.ifhs.ie *Irish Family History Society (Irish Republic)*

www.proni.gov.uk *The Public Record Office of Northern Ireland*

www.nationalarchives.ie *The National Archives of Ireland*

The latter two are the main public records offices if you plan on visiting the archives in person. They are to be found in Belfast and Dublin respectively.

CHAPTER 13

American Research

General Overview

Perhaps you are a Brit with ancestors who were born across the Atlantic, or perhaps you are an American citizen who is interested in tracing your British roots.

Whatever your reason for delving into American genealogy, this research brings its own set of challenges. In many ways it can be easier, as there are many online records, which can be more enlightening than some of the British documents that are available. However, historically the country was not a great keeper of records and much of what was recorded was done so on a local or State level, which leads to little cohesion.

America was colonised by the Europeans from the 16th century onwards and although the first countries to establish colonies were Spain and France, for the purpose of this text, I will focus on British migrants.

As expected, Ancestry and Find My Past are two of the best sources. In both cases it is necessary to have a higher subscription in order to obtain the relevant records.

In the 19th century there were countless books written by Americans that traced their ancestry, often back to their arrival in the country and beyond. Ancestry has many of these gems in their "North America, Family Histories" section. If you search for a name on the home page and find one of these pages, it may prove very useful. I like to take it one step further and find the complete text of the original work, which is searchable, as often one piece of information can lead to another. The best way to do this is to copy the title of the actual book from Ancestry and paste it into your search engine. It is likely that somewhere on that first page you will come across the book on the website https://archive.org.

This is one of my favourite resources for all out-of-copyright literature. The majority of books are of American origin, but there are many thousands of other nations available. This is a completely free resource, simply click on the 'search inside' button and by typing in a keyword or name, the required pages will be flagged up at the bottom of the screen.

As well as these personal genealogies, there are many other books on Ancestry, and Find My Past which give details of British immigrants, including those 'in bondage' that were convicted criminals sent to America before it gained independence.

AMERICAN RESEARCH

Convicts sent to America

From 1615 to 1775, it is estimated that more than fifty thousand British convicts, not only men, but also women and children, were sent to America, mostly to Virginia and Maryland. It has also been estimated that almost ten per cent of migrants during this time were British convicts. Many were sent for petty crimes or for being in debt, in fact apart from murder that was always punishable by hanging, they could be transported for any misdemeanor or felony. They were sent for a period of seven to fourteen years, but as with the later transportation to Australia, they rarely returned to Britain once their time was up. Trying to escape back to Britain was punishable by death.

The convicts were often put to manual labour, such as agriculture, particularly tobacco production or in times of war recruited as soldiers. Others were sold to tradespersons.

Convicts chained together on their way to the ship

Many did not make it across the Atlantic, and it is estimated that about five thousand died on their way, commonly from smallpox and typhus and occasionally from starvation.

In 1670 the Virginian authorities passed an act that prohibited the arrival of convicts, but the King overruled them, which led to disquiet amongst the free settlers. By the end of the 17th century colonial ports began refusing to accept convict ships, which had previously relied on merchants using their own vessels. So, in 1718 the Transportation Act was passed in Britain, which subsidised the ships through a network of merchants.

This caused more unrest in the colonies and in 1732 the colony of Georgia was established (named after George II), for petty criminals and debtors. As well as ridding Britain of undesirables, and freeing up space in overcrowded prisons, it also made the government money, as the convicts were sold to plantation owners as indentured servants who had to work out their time for their new bosses.

Virginia continued to pass laws to prevent the influx of convicts, which the Crown continued to overturn, but by the beginning of the American Revolution, colonial ports had all but ceased accepting convict ships and the last boatload arrived on the James River in 1776.

After Independence some who had served their term did return to Britain, but many remained in the New World and became honest citizens.

If you are trying to trace relatives that were transported to America then a good place to start is at Ancestry where you will find The Complete Book of Emigrants in Bondage, 1614–1775. There are also other useful records such as Middlesex, England, Convict Transportation Contracts, 1682–1787.

There are literally millions of other records on the two main websites including censuses, military records, passenger lists, births, marriages and deaths. Many of the states have detailed records, but like our counties, some are more complete than others. Most of the New England states and Pennsylvania are particularly well documented, as most of the early settlers there were Quakers from Europe who kept detailed and accurate records.

Another excellent source of many American records is familysearch.org. This is a free site which gives access to millions of records worldwide.

Religious 'Freedom' in America – Quakers, Pilgrims and Puritans

The Religious Society of Friends, also known as Quakers, was a group founded in England in the 17th century by shoemaker George Fox who grew to believe that the presence of God was within people and not in conventional places of worship. He was first jailed for blasphemy in 1650 and returned to prison on many occasions.

Quakers were persecuted for their beliefs. They chose simple ceremonies and had no official clergy. They believed in equality of the sexes and were pacifists. Quakers first arrived in America in the 1650s. Eventually they would play a key role in both the abolition of slavery and women's rights movements.

However, early on an estimated seventy per cent of them owned slaves, a practice that was banned for all Quakers by the 1780s.

The first Quaker in America was probably Elizabeth Harris, who visited Virginia and Maryland. By the early 1660s, more than fifty other Quakers had followed her. Some still faced persecution in some colonies such as Massachusetts where four Quakers were executed by Puritans.

In 1681, William Penn was given a large land grant in America to pay off a debt owed to his family. Penn went on to found Pennsylvania as a sanctuary for religious freedom and tolerance. Within just a few years, several thousand Friends had moved to Pennsylvania from Britain. Many were involved in the colony's government and were quite powerful, which sometimes conflicted with their beliefs.

When looking at Quaker records it needs to be remembered, that prior to 1752, the calendar was different. For example, when you see '5th month', this means July not May.

AMERICAN RESEARCH

Below is an example of a Quaker marriage record.

The Quakers were not the first to seek religious freedom in America. In 1620, one hundred and two Puritan Separatists set out for America. They were unlike most Puritans because they wanted a complete break from the Church of England. Originally, they had fled to the more tolerant Netherlands, but fearing they would lose their cultural identity they set out for the New World and founded the Plymouth Colony in Massachusetts.

Unlike the Separatists, other Puritans did not want to break from the Church of England; they wanted to 'purify' it. In 1629 Charles II granted a royal charter for the establishment of the Massachusetts Bay Colony. Between then and 1640 over thirteen thousand men, women and children sailed to Massachusetts. During this time and after, several factions of the religion evolved, and the movement spread across New England founding colonies in Rhode Island, Connecticut and New Hampshire.

With all these religious groups, the relationships between them and the Native Americans was complex. Depending on which text you refer to, there were periods of harmony and mutual respect, but also disharmony, massacre and war. For the purpose of this narrative, I leave it to the interested reader to conduct their own research.

It was not only ex-convicts and religious groups that sailed to America from Britain. As well as indentured servants there were those who had sufficient means to pay their own passage and chose to make the journey to the New World for financial gain.

Economic Migrants

Indentured servants emigrated to America under contract to work between five and seven years in exchange for their passage. It is estimated that up to eighty per cent of migrants travelling to America at this time fell into this category, to take their chance on a new life in America.

Others who either had the means or were able to save for the journey, travelled in anticipation of a better life. The journey was dangerous, but the English way was changing with the privatisation of shared pastures and farmlands, which caused prices of essentials to increase dramatically. More than half of the English peasantry was landless.

Many of these economic migrants settled in the more southern states of Virginia and the Carolinas, but countless died within a year of arrival of diseases like dysentery, typhoid, and malaria. For the majority, their life was not so bountiful as the religious settlers.

In 1691 the Headright System was introduced. Headrights were granted by the London Virginia company giving fifty acres of land to colonists who paid their own way to Virginia or paid the way for someone else to go. The prospect of owning land, an impossible dream in England, was an even greater incentive for English emigration to America.

Over the following two centuries many travelled from England, Ireland, Scotland and Wales to find a better life in America. By the 19th century this number had decreased with British economic migrants choosing Canada or Australia, who by then had better prospects and more favourable immigration policies. For Scottish roots try 'The Original Scots Colonists of Early America, 1612–1783' in Ancestry. There are also several other useful Scottish collections including 'Scots in New England, 1623–1873', 'Scots in the USA and Canada, 1825–1875', 'Scots in the American West, 1783-1883' and 'Scots in the Mid-Atlantic States, 1783–1883'.

Slavery

English immigration to America also saw the introduction of slavery to the colonies. The first black Africans to come to America during this period came as indentured servants. However, almost all the Africans who followed came as chattelled slaves.

These men, women and children were sometimes forcibly taken from their homes, but more usually were sold by their tribal chiefs. This was to increase the profits made on the tobacco plantations. Twenty black African slaves were first brought to Jamestown, Virginia in 1619. The census of 1790 showed that the number of slaves had rocketed to over six hundred and ninety-four thousand. This was nearly one in four of the entire population.

Finding Birth, Marriage and Death Records

Unlike UK records, finding vital documents from America is more a matter of luck. Records vary from State to State and, before the 20th century, records were not always kept. However, some can be found in local register books and some in religious records. The latter is particularly good in the New England States and Pennsylvania, where early Quaker statistics are very well documented. By the 20th century it became more common to issue certificates, with each State developing its own laws, but even these can be sketchy at times.

The truth is that by searching the old favourites like Ancestry, Find My Past and familysearch.org you may find what you are looking for. Chances are if the records are not available there, then they don't exist. However, some States are yet to place their records online.

To find out more visit:

www.familysearch.org/blog/en/online-united-states-birth-marriage-death-records.

US Censuses

The first Federal Population Census was taken in 1790 and has been taken every ten years since. In America, as in the UK, there is a restriction on access to more recent data. However, there is a seventy-two-year restriction, so records are available up until 1950.

From 1850 details were provided for all individuals and give invaluable information such as age, country of birth, value of their home, their occupation, crops they grew and much more. This information varies from year to year. Much of the 1890 census was destroyed by fire, so there are very limited records available. Prior to 1850, only the head of household was listed and the number of household members in selected age groups.

These censuses are available as transcripts on familysearch.org, but you can view the original images on Ancestry and Find My Past. As well as the Federal Censuses there are also various State Censuses available. As usual, just type in a name, date and place if known and see what comes up.

Other Useful Resources

Newspapers.com which is linked to Ancestry is a particularly good source of American newspapers as well as other parts of the world. This requires a subscription, although there is a 7-day free trial period.

There are several free websites which can lead to additional information. These include:

http://fultonhistory.com which has millions of pages of historic newspapers from America and Canada

http://africanaheritage.org which holds records on former slaves, freedpersons and their descendants.

http://immigrants.byu.edu which has emigration registers for locating birthplaces of immigrants in their native countries.

These free websites are increasing in number and a particularly good place to find them is:

https://familyhistorydaily.com/genealogy-resources/50-free-genealogy-sites

CHAPTER 14

Canadian Research

General Overview

In 1534 Jacques Cartier arrived on the shores of Canada and claimed the land in the name of the King of France. He named the lands that he explored 'Canada' after the native Iroquois word 'Kanata' meaning village.

Attempts were made in the subsequent decades to establish French settlements, but it wasn't until 1608 when Samuel de Champlain planted a Fleur-de-lis flag near what is now Place Royale in Quebec City, that the French began to settle in any number. This was not without its challenges. The harsh climate and the resentment of the native population had a negative impact.

Jacques Cartier

Colonization continued, but their numbers did not increase significantly. This was partly because they were more interested in trading than colonization, and by 1763 when the territory was ceded to Great Britain, the French population only numbered sixty-five thousand. Today there is still a large population of French speaking people who descended from those original pioneering and hardy settlers.

Immigration from Britain began, mainly from Scotland, Ireland and the North of England. Many Irish were fleeing from severe economic circumstances, and settled in Newfoundland, then later to Nova Scotia and Prince Edward Island.

In 1745 there was a break-up in the clan system in Scotland and this led to a considerable influx of new settlers, although at this time the preferred destination was still the American colonies. However, after the American War of Independence, Canada became more desirable and an estimated fifty thousand British Loyalists, including those who had fought

Fur traders in Canada trading with Native Americans in 1777

in the Revolutionary War, fled to Canada from the Colonies. As European immigration increased there was a significant decrease in the number of native Americans. Estimates state that from a population of two million in the early 17th century they numbered as little as a hundred thousand by the mid-19th century.

The influx of British immigrants continued, but by 1837 there was a call for an Independent Canada and on the 1st of July 1867 the British North America Act established the Dominion of Canada as a self-governing entity within the British Empire.

When Alberta and Saskatchewan were established in 1905, settlers from the US accounted for the largest single group of immigrants. Some of these were African Americans fleeing persecution in Oklahoma. There were also Polish, Dutch, German, Finnish and Scandinavian immigrants who, finding the US an expensive place to settle, moved on to Canada.

During the 20th century, many other nations chose Canada as a new place to start over. By 1911, more than one in five of Canada's population had been born outside of the country.

There are now ten Canadian provinces (the equivalent of a state in America) and three territories to the north. The provinces are Alberta, British Columbia, Manitoba, New Brunswick, Newfoundland and Labrador, Nova Scotia, Ontario, Prince Edward Island, Quebec, and Saskatchewan.

The territories are Northwest Territories, Nunavut, and Yukon.

The difference between a province and a territory has to do with their governance. While provinces exercise constitutional powers in their own right, the territories exercise delegated powers under the authority of the Parliament of Canada.

Convicts Transported to Canada

France had been transporting convicts to Canada since the mid-16th century, with some measure of success. They were mainly common criminals, (no political or religious criminals were transported) and they were used as forced labour. This policy freed up space in the jails and made economic sense. However, Britain even after the American War of Independence, chose Australia as a preferred destination.

There were a few attempts to transport convicts to Canada, but in 1769 when more than a hundred were sent to St John's in Newfoundland from Dublin, the authorities could not cope with an influx of so many starving, diseased and sometimes dangerous men, so the idea was abandoned. Ironically, in the mid-19th century, Canada was sending their own convicts to Australia.

Home Children

From the late 1860s and for the next eighty or so years, over one hundred thousand children were sent to Canada from the British Isles. Only about two per cent of these children were actually orphans, many came from families who had fallen on hard times due to illness or the death of a parent. The workhouses were overcrowded and sending these children to a cleaner and healthier environment seemed to the authorities the ideal solution. Many parents never saw their children again.

The children were sent mainly by charitable organisations such as Barnardos and the Salvation Army. They came to be known as Home Children, due to the many coming from Children's Homes.

In Canada they were employed in agricultural and domestic work. They were popular amongst Canadians as they were a cheap source of labour and there were reportedly at least seven applications for every child. Many parents were relieved that their offspring would be getting a better life, but the truth was that the monitoring of placements was not rigorously applied, and many were neglected, abused and overworked. Often siblings were separated, and many children ran away and some even committed suicide.

Dr. Barnardo Children having their trunks inspected before leaving for Canada on the Duchess of York, April 19, 1929

The stigma of being what was known as a Home Boy or Home Girl was a source of shame and many carried the truth of their origins all their lives. It is estimated that over ten per cent of Canadians are descended from Home Children, a fact which many are unaware of.

During the First World War, many Home Boys enlisted hoping to get home to visit their families. Some lied about their age to achieve this end.

However, although many were treated poorly, others thrived and ended up living happy, healthy and more prosperous lives than they might have done had they stayed in Britain.

Slavery

Enslavement in New France (as the French held territories of North America were known), began in the early 17th century and initially involved the indigenous population, who were treated as property by the colonists. The settlers also traded with the Caribbean slave owners obtaining goods produced by the slaves there. In time they became involved in the private buying of black African slaves.

Slave ownership was not just confined to elite society. Those from all walks of life including tradesman, merchants, innkeepers and even the clergy and nuns bought and utilised enslaved men, women and children.

In 1760 when Britain defeated the French, there was a specific clause in the Articles of Capitulation, the treaty that was signed at the surrender of Montreal. Article XLVII stated:

> "The Negroes and panis [indigenous slaves] of both sexes shall remain, in their quality of slaves, in the possession of the French and Canadians to whom they belong; they shall be at liberty to keep them in their service in the colony, or to sell them; and they may also continue to bring them up in the Roman Religion."

This clause ensured that the right to buy and sell slaves remained a legal right.

The number of enslaved Africans in British North America increased significantly after the American War of Independence. White Americans were encouraged to move north, and the Imperial Statute of 1790 allowed settlers to bring 'negros [sic], household furniture, utensils of husbandry, or cloathing [sic]' duty-free.

Many slaves tried to escape, even though the punishment if they were caught would have been harsh, sometimes even death.

Some slave owners granted them their freedom in their Wills, on occasion leaving them goods or even land, but others bequeathed the slaves to family and friends, just like any other property.

"Allegorical illustration of a slave's transition to liberty as he escapes his owner and is embraced by an Abolitionist in a Free State" Engraving taken from the book, 'Narrative of the Life and Adventures of Henry Bibb, An American Slave', 1849.

Attempts were made to abolish slavery, backed by the growing abolition movement in Britain. Some laws were passed in certain territories that limited the power of the slave owners, such as the 1793 Act to Limit Slavery, which limited the time that formally enslaved persons were bound to service to just nine years. However, it was not until the 1830s that slavery was completely abolished throughout British North America.

Where to Find Canadian Records

In Canada there are basically four major types of records on the national level: census records, immigration, naturalisation and military records. Many early records are scant or non-existent and on a provincial level only Quebec and Ontario go back to the early days of British settlement. As with America, birth, marriage and death records are found at provincial or state level.

Ancestry has a wide selection of information such as the "U.S. and Canada, Passenger and Immigration Lists Index, 1500s-1900s" and a variety of national and provincial censuses. They also have military records and a good amount of documentation from Quebec and Ontario, including parish records.

Find My Past is more useful in finding newspaper articles, but also holds military records. Familysearch.org has many links to useful publications.

If you are looking for information on the Home Children, then an excellent site is at http://www.bac-lac.gc.ca, the Library and Archives Canada (LAC) which holds 'unique and extensive records including passenger lists, Immigration Branch correspondence files and inspection reports, non-government collections such as the Middlemore Home Funds, as well as indexes to some records held in the United Kingdom. The records also include names of older boys and girls who were recruited by immigration agents in the U.K. for farming and domestic work in Canada.'

One other useful source is the British National Archives which has an abundance of information including a very informative audio and video of a talk by Michael Leclerc who is a noted genealogical author, editor, and presenter.

CHAPTER 15

Caribbean Research

General Overview

n the 2001 British census, five hundred and sixty-five thousand, eight hundred and seventy-six people in the United Kingdom reported their ethnicity as 'Black Caribbean'. This number has inevitably been diluted with mixed race marriages over time, so those in Britain with African heritage, who may not even be aware of it, must number countless more. If you are trying to trace your Caribbean roots, whether of African or European origin, then there are many useful resources available.

The 'first' Caribbeans

People have lived in the Caribbean for thousands of years. The main two races in the early 16th century, when Europeans began to arrive on the shores, were the Tainos (often called Arawaks) who settled in the Windward and Leeward Islands and then the Greater Antilles and the Bahamas, and the Caribs who lived throughout the Lesser Antilles. The

Tainos (which means 'peace') were a very spiritual people. They worshipped gods and embraced the natural forces such as rain, wind and fire. To them 'coyaba' (the afterlife) was a land of dancing, without sickness or hunger.

Caribs

The Caribs however, were less religious, and were much more aggressive and proficient hunters, with a more efficient way of cultivating their crops. They were a warrior tribe and wore body paint and their victim's teeth as necklaces.

European Dominance

The Caribs began to systematically force the Tainos from their lands, but it was not until the Spanish arrived in the early 16th century in search of gold, that they were completely wiped out in fewer than fifty years. At first, they had been forced to work in the mines, but when a more productive source of gold was discovered in Mexico, they were no longer needed. Many Spanish settlers moved to Mexico and South America, and the English and French began to colonise the islands. At first, the Caribs continued trying to assert their identity by fighting for land and political rights. In the course of many wars between them and the Europeans and also the Europeans fighting against each other, the islands were continually changing hands.

Servants and White Slaves

The Spanish, Dutch, French and British all wanted to own the islands that could bring them wealth and status. Eventually the Caribs were subdued, their numbers diminished by the superior forces of the Europeans, and as things settled, plantation owners began to use indentured servants for their labour force. These servants often came voluntarily, selling their labour for a period of years in exchange for a small plot of land. Others were not willing participants; some being tricked into believing they were to be indentured. whilst instead being sold as slaves.

Others were simply kidnapped, forced on to slave ships and sent across the ocean. This last practice was particularly predominant in Ireland with over fifty thousand people being sold into slavery. They were treated brutally, and only about fifty percent made it to the end of their servitude.

Transportation

From the 1620s, as well as the willing servants and the white 'slaves', others were transported and used as forced labour. Some were merely 'rogues or vagrants' and went willingly in return for not facing trial, but most were convicted criminals. Between 1660 and 1718, when the authorities refused to take any more, over thirteen thousand convicts were shipped to Jamaica alone.

During the English Civil War, the Jacobite uprisings and other conflicts of the time, political prisoners were also transported to the Caribbean, this included religious rebels such as Quakers and Scottish Covenanters. They were treated harshly and just as other unwilling migrants, they often died on route or later of neglect and disease.

Pirates

In the early 17th century pirate ships were common in Caribbean waters. Some pirates settled in Hispaniola and worked in the cattle trade. They cured their beef in ovens known as 'boucans' and became known as 'buccaneers'. These Brethren of the Coast as they referred to themselves, consisted of small communities of former indentured slaves, deserters and others who had fallen by the wayside. Some made their eventual home in Tortuga off the coast of Haiti, and from here they sent out their ships to pirate the high seas.

A woodcut of Jack Rackham (known as Calico Jack) from Charles Johnson's 1725 edition of "A General History of the Pyrates".

The African Slave Trade

At first, as in the American colonies, the Europeans developed tobacco plantations, but it soon became clear that sugar was more sought after and profitable.

By this time, the indigenous Caribbeans had been virtually wiped out, and during the 18th century the slave trade developed, where African men, women and children, who were either stolen or bought from their tribal leaders, were transported as cargo and used to work on the plantations.

The slaves were packed tightly into the ship's hold, many dying on route. Those who survived were auctioned in the slave market.

The Triangular Trade as it was known, involved shipping goods, such as guns and brandy to Africa in exchange for slaves. The slaves were then taken across the Atlantic to sell in the Caribbean and North America. Then the ships returned to Europe with cargoes of rum and sugar.

It is estimated that between the years 1640 and 1807 more than one and a half million people were taken from Africa to the Caribbean.

Slaves were forced to adopt European culture and language, and many were treated severely and didn't survive long in their new environment. Rebellion saw harsh punishment, and it was legal to kill an African man until the beginning of the 19th century.

In the late 18th century, Britain sent in the military to defend against invasion by competing European nations, and to quell anti-slavery movements, but in 1807 a law was passed in Britain banning the trade of slaves on British ships. However, it was not until 1834 that slavery in British Colonies was abolished altogether.

To compensate the slave owners, there was to be a period of apprenticeship of four or six years during which planters had the right to the continuing labour of their ex-slaves, unless the slaves bought their freedom. The only exception to this was children under six and slaves in the Bahamas and Antigua who were freed immediately.

In addition to this, slave owners were given a total of £20,000,000 in compensation, money which was not ploughed back into the Caribbean economy, instead often being invested in British bonds and property.

The abolition of slavery in the Caribbean by the rest of Europe extended over almost a century, the first abolition being in French held Haiti in 1793 and the last by the Spanish in Cuba in 1886.

Asian immigrants

With the decline of the slave trade during the 19th century, Indians and Chinese migrated to the Caribbean to work as indentured servants on the plantations. The Chinese settled mainly in Jamaica, Trinidad, British Guiana (now Guyana) and later, Cuba. From 1838 to 1917, over half a million Indians from the former British Raj and Colonial India, were taken to British Guiana, Jamaica, Trinidad and Tobago, Martinique, French Guiana, Guadeloupe, Grenada, St. Lucia, St. Vincent, St. Kitts, St. Croix, Suriname and Nevis. It is estimated that about two and a half million Caribbeans can trace at least a part of their lineage back to their Indian roots. Those with Chinese origins are significant, but far fewer than the Indians, as many of them moved on to North America.

Researching your Caribbean Roots

Before slavery was abolished, it is not always easy to trace someone's African roots. They were often forbidden to attend the Anglican church, so are not listed in the usual church registers for birth, marriage and death. Towards the end of the 18th century, non-conformist churches began to emerge which welcomed the enslaved community. From about 1820 the Anglicans began to relax their rules also, so if you are lucky, there may be something to find.

It was common for the slave women to have children by their masters, and procreation, whether by other slaves or the master was encouraged as this meant freer labour. Because so many of these children were born out of wedlock, if they were given a surname at all, they often took the mother's name, which was rarely the same as their African ancestors, but a name chosen, by themselves or their owners. After they were freed, they sometimes took on the name of their father, whether that was their former owner or another slave.

From here on, with freedom, whether granted before or after the abolition, there is a greater likelihood of finding records. A trip to the Caribbean to search their archives and libraries would be the best way to achieve this, but some records are available online.

Employment records, wills, land registries and many other sources might give clues to your ancestor's line, but again, local records are the most likely to have this information. If you know a birthplace then it is worth contacting the relevant archive by emailing them, to see if they can help.

As slaves were considered property, it is sometimes possible to find information from the slave owners' records. Wills might be particularly useful if slaves were bequeathed or freed. These are not easy to find, but it might be worth looking for slave owners with the same surname.

Slave registers were completed between 1813 and 1834. The earliest are from Trinidad, but other countries didn't pass laws to establish them until much later. These records give valuable information such as approximate age, place of birth and colour (black/negro implies pure African descent, mulatto that of mixed race, usually meaning a European father). There may be dates of birth, mother's name and other useful information.

The best source of information on the main websites is on Ancestry. The resources include registers of some English settlers, with records of baptisms, marriages, burials, wills and probates. Barbados is particularly well documented.

CARIBBEAN RESEARCH

There are also records of the original Scots colonists. Slave records include slave registers of former British Colonial Dependencies from 1813–1834.

Familysearch.org is also a useful source. The records include civil registration in Jamaica from 1880 to 1999, Barbados church records from 1637 to 1887 and much more. If you know the country, just click on the map and follow the links.

Some records are held at the National Archives. They have some good information about Caribbean history and what is available at:

http://www.nationalarchives.gov.uk/caribbeanhistory/movement-of-people.htm

If you believe your ancestor may have been transported, then 'Emigrants in Bondage' on Ancestry, as mentioned in the chapter on America, lists British convicts who were transported to all the colonies.

Finally, if you have ever wondered whether your ancestors were slave owners, then check out www.ucl.ac.uk/lbs. This is an ongoing project which lists slave owners who were granted compensation when slavery was abolished and a list of all the estates in the British Caribbean.

CHAPTER 16

Europe

General Overview

For European family research, there are many online resources at your disposal. Ancestry has birth, marriage and death records of France, Germany, Spain, Italy, Sweden, Denmark, Norway and others. The downside here if you are not bilingual, is that most of the records are in their original language, although this doesn't present too much of a problem as names and dates translate well.

Ancestry also holds many other records and publications that may be worth looking at. The best way to search is to go to the card catalogue and type in the country's name, making sure the box underneath is not checked.

Familysearch.org also holds some interesting material, and a feature I particularly like on their website is the map on the front page which you can click on to find information and records from your desired country.

Of course, you can always look for a country or region's own genealogy websites. Again, the usefulness and availability of these vary greatly. In my experience it is often difficult to obtain specific information and contacting them via email, often receives no response.

As with so much of this kind of research, it really is sometimes the luck of the draw. With so much information being added to the internet every day, the information throughout this book, although still very relevant, is not exhaustive. What you can't find today, look for again in the future.

In Conclusion

Hopefully by now you have begun your research and have discovered some interesting information about your ancestors. Perhaps shocking, perhaps surprisingly comforting, but almost certainly fascinating.

Don't forget to periodically return to any unsolved mysteries and check again on your favourite websites. Subscribe to the newsletters on these sites, as they often send updates on new collections. Look out for new websites that may hold more information and don't be afraid to email organisations or individuals who may have more detailed knowledge of your ancestors. You may get no response, or you may get the answer to that all-important question that has been holding up your research.

One final thing –

This is a journey. Don't anticipate the destination, just enjoy the ride!

INDEX

Abolition of slavery, 156
Act for Relief of The Poor 1597, 75
Act to Limit Slavery 1793, 149
Adoption, 13
African Slave Trade, 155
American census, 140
American War of Independence, 143
American research, 129
American revolution, 132
Anglo-Saxon Society, 45
Apprenticeships, 106, 110
Archives, 6
Aristocracy, 47, 53
Asian Immigrants, 156
Australia, 15, 69, 131

Baptists, 30
Barnardos, 146
Bedlam, 87
Birth Certificates, 10
Black Death, 74, 84, 85
Bow Street Runners, 66
Boys Farm Home, 111, 112
British Army, 59, 63
British Convicts, 131
British National Archives, 150
British North America Act 1867, 144
Bubonic plague, 84

Canada, 116, 142
Caribbean, 151
Caribs, 152
Celtic society, 44
Censuses, 17, 52, 119
Chimney sweeps cancer, 91
Cholera, 88, 92
Church of England, 30, 136
Church of Scotland, 123
Civil war 88
Clandestine marriages, 31
Class System, 44
Commonwealth, 29
Commonwealth War Graves Commission, 63
Compulsory education, 104
Convicts, 69, 131, 145
County Records Office, 7
Covid, 95
Crime, 66
Criminal records, 70
Criminal Amendment Act 1875, 80
Cuba, 156

Death Certificates, 10, 12, 93
Denmark, 160
Disease Prevention Act 1883, 81
Dissolution of the Monasteries 28
Dr Barnardos, 13, 146

East Sussex Records Office, 5
Economic migrants, 137
Education, 100
Education Act 1870, 105
Edward The Confessor, 89
Elementary Education (Blind and Deaf Children) Act 1893), 105
England and Wales Criminal Registers, 70
English Civil War, 29, 95, 153
Enumeration Districts, 23
Europe, 160
Ex-Convicts, 69, 136

Family History Societies, 5, 6
Federal Population Census 1790, 140
Feudal system, 46
First World War, 59, 60, 92
Fleet Marriage, 31
France, 160

Geographical Mobility, 114
Gentry, 28, 47
Germany, 160
Gilbert Unions, 78
Government Record Office, 11
Great Famine, 85
Great Fire of London, 88
Great Plague, 85

Hardwicke's Marriage Act 1753, 31
Highland Family History Society, 121
Home Children, 145, 146
Husbandmen, 47

Illegitimacy, 73
Industrial Revolution, 36, 54, 90, 115
Infant mortality rates, 95
Independent Schools, 101
Industrial Schools Act 1857, 103
Internet, 1, 2
Ireland, 120, 126
Italy, 160

Jacobite Uprisings, 153
Jewish ancestors, 118

Kelly's Directories, 55
King Charles 2nd, 58

Landed Gentry, 53
Last Will and Testament, 56
Local Archives, 7
London Apprentice Abstracts, 55
London, England School Admission Discharges 1840–1914, 111
London Poor Law Records, 82
London School Boards, 104
Lunatic, 18

Malaria, 90
Marriage, 28
Marriage Certificate, 10, 11, 12
Mary Tudor, 29
Merchant Navy Apprenticeship Records, 113
Metropolitan Police, 67
Mexico, 152
Middle Ages, 83
Middle Classes, 53
Military, 58
Military Records, 63

INDEX

NATO, 58
National Archives, 6, 22
National Health Service, 54, 79
National Records of Scotland, 120
National School Register 1870–1914, 111
New Zealand, 116
Non-Conformist, 30, 31
Norman conquest, 45
Norway, 160

Official Registration of Adoptions, 13
Oliver Cromwell, 59
Online parish records, 35
Outdoor Relief Prohibition Order 1844, 79

Parish records, 33, 61
Peasants, 45
Peels factory Act 1802, 107
Peelers, 67
Petty criminals, 50, 132
Pilgrims, 133
Plague, 84
Pirates, 154
Polio, 93
Poor Laws, 74, 78
Poor Law Amendment Act 1834, 79
Poor Relief Act 1601, 106
Potato Blight, 116
Press gang, 58
Prisons, 69
Prostitutes, 50
Protestants, 30, 181
Public Assistance Institution, 81
Puritans, 136

Quakers, 133, 134
Queen Victoria, 17, 69

Ragged Schools, 103, 111
Relief of the Poor Act 1782, 78
Renaissance, 101
Restoration (The), 59
Rickets, 91
River Police, 66
Romans, 44, 100
Royal Air Force, 60
Royal Navy, 58, 61
Royal Flying Corps, 61

Salvation Army, 146
Scarlet Fever, 89
Scotland, 120
Scottish Association of Family History Societies, 122
Scottish Catholic Archives, 126
Scottish Genealogy Society, 126
Scottish Land Clearances, 116
Second World War, 94
Serfs, 46,
Servants, 136,
Settlement Act 1662, 74
Shopkeepers, 47
Slavery, 138, 147, 153, 155
Slave Registers, 158
Smallpox, 86, 89, 93
Spain, 160
Spanish Flu, 96
Society of Friends, 31
Sunday School, 102, 115
Statute of Artificers and Apprentices 1513, 106
Statute of Cambridge 1388, 74

Statute of Legal Settlement 1547, 75
Sweden, 160

Tax records, 56
Tenant farmers, 47
The Factory Act 1833, 51
The Great Stink, 92
The Library and Archives (LAC) Canada, 150
Thomas Cromwell, 28
Toleration Act of 1689, 30
Transportation Act 1718, 132
Trinidad, 157
Tuberculosis, 86 93
Typhus, 88

United Kingdom Police Gazettes, 71
US Censuses, 140

Vaccines, 93
Vagabonds and Beggars Act 1495, 74
Vagabonds Act 1531, 75
Victorian Society, 50
Viking invasions, 100

Welfare State, 54
White Slaves, 153
Whooping Cough, 93
William Hogarth, 107
William the Conqueror, 45
William Penn, 134
Workhouse, 73, 78
Workhouse Test Act 1723, 78

Yeomans, 48

PAULINE GOLDS
www.bygonelives.com

Pauline Golds is a genealogist and writer living on the south coast of England. Previous literary works consist of a nostalgic stroll through her childhood in 1960s Sussex, as well as an historical novel inspired by a wealth of colourful discoveries made about her ancestors through tracing her own family tree.

From Greyscale to Technicolour and *Silhouettes in a Silent Land* are available to preview and purchase at
www.paulinegolds.com

In her role as a genealogist, Pauline's aim is to give an affordable service to those on a budget. If you are interested in learning more about having research carried out for you or have any questions relating to tracing your own family tree please visit www.bygonelives.com or email pauline@bygonelives.com